NO MORE LIMITS!

UNLEASHING YOUR POTENTIAL IN GOD

by

Happy Caldwell

Harrison House
Tulsa, Oklahoma

No More Limits!
ISBN 1-57794-165-9
Copyright © 1999 by Happy Caldwell
Agape Church
P.O. Box 22007
Little Rock, AR 72221-2007

Published by **Harrison House, Inc**.
P. O. Box 35035
Tulsa, Oklahoma 74153

Acknowledgements

Now unto him that is able to do exceeding abundantly above all that we ask or think, according to the power that worketh in us, Unto him be glory in the church by Christ Jesus throughout all ages, world without end. Amen (Ephesians 3:20-21).

Contents

Contents

Foreword

Prior to May 1954, most of the sports world thought that running a mile in less than four minutes was impossible. Runners had failed for decades to break the four-minute mile barrier. It was seen as an obstacle, both physical and psychological, that exceeded human limits.

However, on May 6, 1954, a medical student at Oxford University named Roger Bannister broke the four-minute-mile barrier, proving that limits can be broken.

The first thing that Bannister did was wonder whether the biggest obstacle runners faced might not be their own beliefs or fears. After all, with better running conditions and better training, someone could possibly run a mile in less than four minutes.

Roger Bannister became fascinated by the challenge of proving the limits were self-imposed. In his book, *The Four-Minute Mile*, he said, "It was like an Everest, a barrier that seemed to defy attempts to break it."

Sound familiar? What about the limits in your life, do they scream back at you and defy your attempt to push them out of your way?

Bannister studied the problem as you would any scientific experiment. That increased his understanding of the common sense of it. He read up on the physiology of breaking the barrier and confirmed in himself that it was possible.

When we renew our minds with the Word of God and hear what the Word says...faith comes. When faith comes…fear goes. Fear knocks on the door; faith answers and there is no one there. When we identify our limits, we can confront them and overcome them by acting on God's Word.

The man who besought Jesus to deliver his son said, "If you can do anything, have compassion on us and help us." Jesus said, "If you can believe, all things are possible to him that believeth." The man responded with tears and said, "I believe, help thou my unbelief." Unbelief sets limits. When we realize it was our own unbelief that set the limit, we can remove the limit with our faith.

Roger Bannister began building endurance to break the four-minute-mile barrier that had challenged runners for years.

He trained to exhaustion in 30-minute workouts. He cross-trained to build endurance. To strengthen the muscle in the back of his legs, he ran up hill and downhill on grass. One month before the race, he went hiking to clear his head and focus his concentration. Five days before the race, he rested.

The day of the race the weather was less than perfect. In fact, he considered not running. However, "I had prepared and trained; I was at my peak physically and mentally … therefore I made a decision.

Bannister said he refused to give in to crushing fatigue as well as oxygen debt. "My body had long since exhausted all it's energy … but I went on running just the same."

As Bannister lunged forward into the finish line tape, he fell exhausted into outstretched arms and awaited confirmation that he had broken the limit and run a mile in 3:59:04.

By the end of 1955, one year later, four other runners had broken the limit of the four-minute mile.

In this book, you will learn there are no more limits for the child of God. Just as Roger Bannister broke a limit in the natural realm, God has called us to break limits in the spiritual realm.

As we step into a new millennium, God has said, "No More Limits!"

CONQUERING YOUR LIMITS

YOU ARE A NIKE PERSON

* * *

Victory, Conquest and Success

Millions of people are wearing shoes, shirts and hats with a biblical message imprinted on them and they do not even know it. I am talking about people who have bought shoes and clothes with the Nike logo.

"Nike" is a biblical word. The original Greek word translated as "victory" in 1 John 5:4 is "nike," pronounced "nee' kay." This word also means conquest and success.

> **For whatsoever is born of God overcometh the world: and this is the victory (nike) that overcometh the world, even our faith.**
>
> **(1 John 5:4).**

When I discovered the word "nike" in the Bible meant conquest, victory and success, I became excited and went out and bought myself three hats, a pair of tennis shoes and two shirts with the Nike logo on it. If you are looking at me, you are looking at "Nike Man."

If you own sporting apparel from the Nike Corporation, such as a pair of Nike tennis shoes or a Nike hat, you are wearing a symbol of victory. You are wearing something that symbolizes overcoming and being victorious. I am not endorsing the Nike Corporation or their sporting apparel. I am just pointing out what the word "nike" means.

You can tell people the word "nike" is in the Bible and means victory, conquest and success. You can tell them about the real "nike Man," Jesus Christ. Jesus died so we can be victorious in this life and the life to come. Tell them they can be a "nike person" in Jesus.

The Devil Has Been Swooshed

Nike shoes and clothes carry a logo that looks like a checkmark. This mark is called a "swoosh." The meaning of the "swoosh" is basically *leave them in the dust*.

The serpent is symbolic for the devil. In Genesis God cursed the devil:

> **And the LORD God said unto the serpent,**
> **Because thou hast done this, thou art cursed above**
> **all cattle, and above every beast of the field; upon**
> **thy belly shalt thou go, and dust shalt thou eat all**
> **the days of thy life:**
>
> **(Genesis 3:14).**

The serpent in the Garden of Eden was used by the devil. God told the serpent he was going to eat dust. Did you know that the devil has been "swooshed" by God?

1 John 5:4 says, *Whatsoever is born of God overcomes the world.* Jesus overcame the world. He overcame death, hell and everything. He overcame the god of this world, the prince and power of the air. Jesus has overcome it all.

When you accepted Jesus Christ as your Lord, you became an overcomer by becoming part of His family. When you became born again, you were born of God. You have a share in the spoils of Jesus victory over the devil. It is not because of anything you did. In yourself you could not overcome the devil, but through Jesus you share in His victory.

Nike people are victors over the devil through Jesus. Nike people leave the devil in the dust.

Just Do It

The Nike Corporation used to have an advertising slogan, "Just Do It!" The Nike Corporation is not just selling sporting apparel; they are selling an image of success and victory. The Nike Corporation does this by associating their products with winners. When you buy Nike shoes and sporting apparel, the company wants you to feel like you are a winner too. The next time you are out somewhere, look around. You will see that Nike has been very successful in marketing their products. Almost everywhere you go people are wearing Nike tennis shoes, Nike hats and Nike shirts.

Image is important today. People wear all kinds of things to project a successful image. People wear designer clothing and name brand shoes to make a statement. People try to say they have arrived because they are wearing a particular garment or a particular brand of shoes.

People are willing to pay a price to wear the right clothes and shoes. A pair of fancy tennis shoes is expensive. There are also many more styles to choose from than ever before. Stores sell shoes to walk in, shoes to run in, shoes to jog in, shoes to play sports in, and shoes that do not even look like shoes. When you wear the Nike brand, you are identifying with the logo and the image that says, "I am a victor. I am a conqueror. I have arrived."

Identify With Jesus

Our society has more of an understanding of what it means to be a winner through the subtle message of a Nike tennis shoe than they do through the word "Christian." But when we call ourselves Christians, we are born of God and through Jesus we are winners. Through Jesus we are overcomers and have success and victory.

It is good to identify with being a success. It is good for you to identify with being a conqueror and being a victor. God wants you to identify with Jesus. Jesus is a victor. Jesus is a conqueror. Jesus is a success.

The garments on the outside are not important. The important thing is for you to understand who you are in Christ. In Christ you are a super-victor. Wear your Nike gear if you like, but say, "In Jesus, I am a winner! In Jesus, I am an overcomer! In Jesus, I am more than a conqueror! In Jesus, I have arrived!"

God wants you to see a new spiritual image of yourself. He wants you to identify with the victories of Jesus. Jesus overcame hell, death and the grave. He defeated all the enemies we will ever encounter. There is no greater name than the name of Jesus. As a Christian, you are entitled to share in the benefits belonging to Jesus Christ. As a Christian you share in the inheritance of Jesus. Grasp this truth in your mind and you will remove all the limits that are keeping you from doing what God wants you to do.

The Word of God says you are a success through Jesus (2 Corinthians 2:14). It is good to line your thinking up with the Word of God. This is not about the power of positive thinking. It is much more than that. This is about the power of the positive Word of God. When you have the Word of God in you and it begins to renew your mind, it will change you into who God wants you to be. The Word of God in you will make you a victorious overcomer through all the challenges of life.

You can be living a life where there are no limits in what you can do through Jesus. Rejoice in the fact that you are born of God. The Bibles says,

> For whatsoever is born of God overcometh the
> world: and this is the victory (nike) that over-
> cometh the world, even our faith.
>
> (1 John 5:4).

GOD HAS A PLAN FOR YOUR SUCCESS AND VICTORY

* * *

You Have a Divine Destiny

God told the Old Testament prophet Jeremiah that he knew him before he was born.

> Before I formed thee in the belly I knew thee;
> and before thou camest forth out of the womb.
>
> (Jeremiah 1:5).

The book of Romans says God knew you before you were born. Think about this for a moment. Your existence is no accident. God knew you before you were formed in your mother's womb. He had a plan for your life before you were born. God foreknew you and He predestinated you to be conformed to the image of his son Jesus.

> For whom he did foreknow, he also did pre-
> destinate to be conformed to the image of his Son,
> that he might be the firstborn among many
> brethren.
>
> (Romans 8:29).

God has prepared the way for you to be born again, to be saved, to be conformed to the image of Jesus. However, it is up to you whether you will take advantage of what He has prepared for you. God knows all things, but God gives you a choice. He gives you a free will. He gives you the ability to choose. You can seek God and find out His will for your life.

Be assured God has a wonderful plan for your life, but He has also given you the right to choose to be born again.

15

He has also given you the right to choose and seek Him to receive all that He has planned for your life. Jesus made all this possible by His death. Now, it is up to you to make good choices and to follow Him daily.

You are Called, Justified and Glorified

> Moreover whom he did predestinate, them he also called: and whom he called, them he also justified: and whom he justified, them he also glorified.   (Romans 8:30)

God has a predetermined plan for your life. This means God has called you. If God has called you, he has also justified you. When God justified you, He took away all charges against you. He removed your sins and gave you new life in Christ Jesus. You now have the right to go before God with a pure heart. You are justified through the death of Jesus. God gave you a new life in Christ so you can fulfill His plan for your life.

God wants you to take your place with Jesus in heaven. God has glorified you through his grace. You do not deserve to be glorified. Your glory is a reflection of the Glory of God in you. This glory is part of the new nature that comes from accepting Jesus Christ as your Savior and being born again.

It is important to realize God has a plan for your life. God has called you. God has justified you, and God has glorified you through His Son Jesus. God has given you all the necessary ingredients to be successful in this life and forever. This is all accomplished by the grace of God. This is His gift to you.

> Even when we were dead in sins, hath quick-
> ened us together with Christ, (by grace ye are
> saved;) And hath raised us up together, and made
> us sit together in heavenly places in Christ Jesus:
> That in the ages to come he might shew the ex-
> ceeding riches of his grace in his kindness toward
> us through Christ Jesus. For by grace are ye saved
> through faith; and that not of yourselves: it is the
> gift of God.
>
> (Ephesians 2:5-8)

God has called you and God has justified you. He has glorified you and made you to sit with him in heavenly places. Spiritually and legally you have been made to sit with Him in heavenly places.

If God is For You, Who can be Against You?

Our position in Christ in the heavenlies also carries with it some rights here in the earth. God is for you and not against you. God is able to keep you from failing. God wants you to fulfill His predestinated plan for your life. God is on your side. Those who oppose God cannot prevail against the plans God has for you.

The Apostle Paul asks a good question:

> What shall we then say to these things? If God
> be for us, who can be against us?
>
> Romans 8:31

Think about this a moment and give your own reply to this question. How would you respond? What will you say about the fact that God has called, justified and glorified you through His Son, Jesus?

The Apostle Paul gives you the answer. This is an open book test. The answer follows the question. What should we say to these things? He said, *If God be for us, who can be against us?* This is a wonderful promise that applies to you. God is on your side.

Personalize this promise and say it out loud, "If God is for me, who can be against me?"

God's plan for your life includes the security that nobody and nothing can prevail against you when you are fulfilling His divine purpose and destiny for your life.

You Have Been Freely Given All Things

God is on your side. He is not holding back his blessings.

> He that spared not his own Son, but delivered him up for us all, how shall he not with him also freely give us all things?
>
> (Romans 8:32).

This verse says God has freely given you all things. "All things" is not restrictive. "All things" means that there are no limits to what God has freely given you. God's plan for your life is to freely give you all things.

You are a Super-Champion through the Love of Jesus

God has freely given you all things. There is nothing that can happen to you that will keep God's love from you. God loves you and has destined you to be more than a conqueror over the circumstances of life.

> Nay, in all these things we are more than conquerors through him that loved us. (Romans 8:37).

The Greek word for more than a conqueror is a word derived from the same root Greek word for victory, "nike." The verb form of the noun "nike" is "nikao," pronounced "nik-ah'-o."

The Greek verb "nikao" means *to overcome*. The phrase "more than a conqueror" comes from the Greek word "hupernikao," pronounced "hooper-nik-ah'-o." The first part of this word "hupernikao" is the prefix "huper. " The modern equivalent of this is the prefix "hyper." "Hyper" means *more than* or *excessive*. It could also mean *super*. Put the two words together: "hupernikao" means you are a super-overcomer or a super-victor.

When you are born again, you can claim the title of super-victor through Jesus. You are not a super-victor in yourself. You are a super-victor in Jesus. Jesus has already won the victory. You are taking your place along side of Him as the super-victor of the universe.

You are more than a conqueror because Jesus won the victory. You can personalize Romans 8:37 and say it to yourself: "I am more than a conqueror through Him that loved me."

You have the ability to do whatever God has called you to do. God has a wonderful plan for your life. As you begin to study the Word of God, He reveals Himself to you. When you read your Bible prayerfully you begin to understand how much God really wants to bless you and cause you to be victorious in life.

Jesus has already won the victory. You are more than a conqueror through Him that loves you. When you have the Word of God in your heart, it begins to renew your mind and it will change you. When your mind is renewed, you become convinced these things are true. When this happens, your life will never be the same.

Be Persuaded Nothing Can Keep God's Love From You

The Apostle Paul was convinced the love of God was stronger than any opposing circumstances in his life. He said,

> For I am persuaded, that neither death, nor
> life, nor angels, nor principalities, nor powers, nor
> things present, nor things to come, Nor height, nor
> depth, nor any other creature, shall be able to sep-
> arate us from the love of God, which is in Christ
> Jesus our Lord.   (Romans 8:38-39).

Being persuaded means you are strongly convinced. You have settled the issue in your mind and your belief is unshakable. Paul was persuaded there were no circumstances, not even death itself, which could separate him from the love of God in Christ Jesus.

You should also be persuaded you are more than a conqueror over death and all adverse circumstances. Jesus conquered everything, and you have nothing to fear. Angels, principalities, powers, things present, things to come, height, depth — nothing can separate you from the love of God.

Jesus overcame death and hell. Jesus overcame everything in the world. He has overcome the devil, the god of this world. He has overcome it all and there is nothing to fear. Be persuaded that through Jesus you are an overcomer. You have been made more than a conqueror through Jesus who loved you and died for you.

THERE IS NO LIMIT TO WHAT YOU CAN DO
* * *

You Can Do It

There are no limits to what you can accomplish through God working in your life. The Apostle Paul knew the power of God was working in him when he said:

> I can do all things through Christ which
> strengtheneth me.   (Philippians 4:13).

The Apostle Paul was persuaded that Christ was his

strength and he could do all things. This statement applies to you. You can rephrase it and say, "I can do all things through Christ who strengthens me."

Jesus lives in you, and He strengthens you. In your own strength you can do nothing, but in the strength of God, you can do all things. "All things" means there is no limit to what you can do. God has given you everything you need to be successful in accomplishing His purposes in your life. Even though you may be weak, through Jesus Christ there is not limit to what you can do. God wants you to understand He will strengthen you. You have no excuse not to be victorious. Jesus has made it all possible for you.

You are a super-victor in Jesus. His victory is your victory. His life is your life. His peace and His joy are your joy. God has freely given you everything in Christ you need to be victorious. Therefore, there are no limits in fulfilling God's purpose and plan for your life.

Push Your Limits

Push your limits out, as far they will go. Pushing your limits does not mean you are going to do something crazy. God does things decently and in order. Pushing the limits means you do things according to the will of God. Pushing the limit means recognizing God has a divine plan and destiny for your life. Pushing the limits means Jesus has won the victory. All that remains for you to do is to understand the will of God for your life and then walk in the victory that is yours through Jesus Christ.

What can you say to all these things? If God is for you who can be against you? You can be the person God wants you to be. You can be a victorious overcomer. You can go beyond the limits of the world and enter into the abundance of the Kingdom of God. You can do all things through Christ who strengthens you!

Triumphing Over Your Limits

TRIUMPH: CELEBRATING VICTORY
OVER THE ENEMY

* * *

Learning About Triumph from Military Victories

In 1991, a coalition of nations led by the United States triumphed over Iraq in the Persian Gulf War. The war lasted only 100 hours and was a lopsided victory for the United States and its allies. When the troops came home after the war, they were overwhelmed with gratitude for their service to their country. Every town greeted the veterans with large signs of welcome. Yellow ribbons were tied around many trees along streets and highways. These war heroes enjoyed a triumphant homecoming.

The victory in the Persian Gulf helped heal many wounds left open from the Vietnam War. Many Americans bitterly opposed the Vietnam War. Vietnam veterans returned home and were often called murderers and spit upon by war protesters. Vietnam veterans received very little recognition for their service to the nation. The Vietnam War did not end in victory and left our nation divided over the outcome of the war. The lack of a definite victory in Vietnam left many people uneasy about the role of the United States in world affairs.

Unlike Vietnam, the war in the Persian Gulf was seen as a war of good against evil. Iraq's leader Saddam Hussein was despised for his aggressive invasion of his neighboring country, Kuwait. The United States and other nations felt it was important to restore the nation of Kuwait. A massive buildup of armed forces was deployed to the Middle East to fight against Iraq.

The brevity of the Persian Gulf War and the decisive victory gave the United States a renewed attitude about itself. The military was once again seen as an agent of good in an evil world. This shattered the attitudes and limits about the nation and its military that remained after the Vietnam War.

After the victory of the Gulf War, veterans where greeted with an overwhelming support and appreciation for what they had done. They had triumphed over the enemy and were treated as conquering heroes. Americans once again felt good about themselves and their role in world affairs.

The celebrations after the Persian Gulf war were reminiscent of the celebrations after World War II. When the Allies won World War II, the free world celebrated the defeat of the enemy. Heroes were given ticker tape parades. There was great rejoicing and dancing in the streets. There were many open displays of gratitude and thanksgiving because the war was finally over. Good had triumphed over evil.

The time after the victory of World War II ushered in a great period of prosperity and peace. Since the end of the Cold War against communism and the end of the Persian Gulf War, the world has enjoyed a period of peace and prosperity. There are still many hot spots around the world but, for the most part, the modern world is enjoying the benefits of peace. These benefits were brought about by the triumph of the modern military over the enemies of the free world.

You are Triumphant in Christ

Triumph is nothing new. The Romans had great parades after the defeat of their enemies. The word "triumph" in the time of Christ was also a name given to the parade where the captured enemies of the Roman Empire were marched in front of thousands of cheering people. The Roman "triumph" was an ancient form of our modern day ticker-tape parade.

The Apostle Paul used the descriptive language of a military victory parade to describe Jesus' triumph over an evil enemy.

> And having spoiled principalities and powers, he made a show of them openly, triumphing over them in it. (Colossians 2:15).

Jesus died and went to hell and conquered death and the grave. Jesus defeated the enemies of God and he led a victory parade back to heaven. We can only try to imagine what this triumph must have been like. It was surely a greater triumph than any triumph ever seen after any war of men.

Jesus is still triumphant over the enemies of darkness. Jesus has returned to heaven and is seated next to His heavenly father. Jesus is allowing us to share in His triumph over the enemy.

> Now thanks be unto God, which always causeth us to triumph in Christ, and maketh manifest the savour of his knowledge by us in every place.   (2 Corinthians 2:14).

Jesus is allowing us to join in His parade of triumph over the enemy. He is allowing us to live a life of faith and purpose where we can demonstrate His victory and overcome limits in our lives. We are to share in Jesus' triumph and bring glory to God through our words and actions. We are to make known the sweet smell of Jesus' triumph wherever we go.

Jesus has won the victory over the devil, and by faith we can appropriate the spoils of His triumph, as we need them. Grasp what this is all about and you will realize what it means to live a life with no more limits.

KING DAVID'S MEN — FROM DISTRESS TO TRIUMPH

* * *

David Triumphed Over Goliath

Triumph is a theme that runs throughout the Bible. One of the most famous examples is the story of David and Goliath. David killed the Philistine giant Goliath with a stone from his slingshot. David's slingshot should not have brought down a heavily armored giant, but God guided the stone right between the giant's eyes and he fell. David then ran toward the giant, took the giant's sword and cut off his head. David then triumphantly held up the head for everybody to see. With the help of God, David had triumphed over Goliath (1 Samuel 17:1-58).

God enabled David to triumph over his enemy. David's triumphant display of the giant's head was a symbol of our triumph over the devil. Jesus has defeated the giant devil. We are no longer to be afraid of the devil. He has been defeated. Jesus chopped off his head. We need to learn what triumph really means and apply it to our daily lives. Our triumph in Christ means the devil cannot limit us anymore.

Distressed, Discontented and in Debt

We can learn more about triumph by looking into the life of David and his men. When David defeated Goliath, his victory gave him great favor with the Israelites. He received the King's daughter for his wife and he was given a good job working for the King. But David's struggles were not over. The King became jealous of David's success and he decided to kill David. King Saul's threats caused David to leave and run for his life. David ended up in a cave in the wilderness.

The following passage of Scripture tells what happened next:

> David therefore departed thence, and escaped to the cave Adullam: and when his brethren and all his father's house heard it, they went down thither to him. And every one that was in distress, and every one that was in debt, and every one that was discontented, gathered themselves unto him; and he became a captain over them: and there were with him about four hundred men.
>
> (1 Samuel 22:1-2).

Try to imagine this picture. David is hiding in a cave. King Saul and his army are chasing him and trying to kill him. David cries out to God to help him, and whom does God send to him? People who are worse off than he is — people in debt, people in distress and people that are discontented. All the people who were in counseling and therapy went to where David was, but that was not the worst of it. He became a captain over them.

God gave David men who were distressed, discontented and in debt. These men may have looked like failures, but God had great plans for them. David did not stay in trouble and neither did these men.

David was a man after God's own heart. David loved God. David also had great faith. All you have to do is read the many Psalms David wrote to see how much he trusted and loved God. God had a plan for David and these 400 men. God took the faithfulness of David and eventually made him King instead of King Saul. When you look to God for your help, no matter how bad your situation becomes, God has a better plan for your life.

Transformed into Mighty Men

Look at what the Bible has to say about David's men after David became the King of Israel.

> These be the names of the mighty men whom David had: The Tachmonite that sat in the seat, chief among the captains; the same was Adino the Eznite: he lift up his spear against eight hundred, whom he slew at one time. And after him was Eleazar the son of Dodo the Ahohite, one of the three mighty men with David, when they defied the Philistines that were there gathered together to battle, and the men of Israel were gone away: He arose, and smote the Philistines until his hand was weary, and his hand clave unto the sword: and the LORD wrought a great victory that day; and the people returned after him only to spoil.
>
> (2 Samuel 23:8-12).

What a great transformation! In a few years time, David's men went from being discontented, depressed, distressed and indebted to being honored as mighty men. They overcame the limits of their circumstances and became triumphant and honored men in the service of King David. This passage of the Bible depicts David's men not as weak men with limiting problems but as mighty men.

God helped David establish the nation of Israel as a powerful kingdom. David established the kingdom and left his son, Solomon, a vast fortune. David ushered in an era that could be called "Israel's Golden Age." David, with God's help, was able to triumph over his enemies and establish a great kingdom which gave glory to God.

Removing Some Limits Takes Time

David's success did not come all at once. David struggled for years to before he triumphed over all his enemies. He killed Goliath while he was a teenager, but it was not until he was thirty years old that he became King over all of Israel (2 Samuel 5:4).

It may take years before you triumph over some limits in your life. Patience and continued diligence is important in the process of removing limits and overcoming obstacles. It is good to remember that many changes do not occur overnight. Many changes occur over a period of time.

David loved God tremendously. It was David's love for God that sustained him during his struggles. David is a good example for us to follow. If you continue to be faithful and love God, you will eventually see the limits in your lives removed. Loving God and continuing to serve God faithfully will eventually cause you to triumph over your limits.

The Faith Hall of Fame

The exploits of King David and other great men of faith are recorded in the Bible to encourage you. The following verses from the Book of Hebrews are part of what I like to call the Faith Hall of Fame:

> And what shall I more say? for the time would fail me to tell of Gedeon, and of Barak, and of Samson, and of Jephthae; of David also, and Samuel, and of the prophets: Who through faith subdued kingdoms, wrought righteousness, obtained promises, stopped the mouths of lions, Quenched the violence of fire, escaped the edge of the sword, out of weakness were made strong, waxed valiant in fight, turned to flight the armies of the aliens. Women received their dead raised to life again: and others were tortured, not accepting deliverance; that they might obtain a better resurrection.... (Hebrews 11:32-38).

Make My Day

Clint Eastwood played a rogue cop in the movie Dirty Harry. He had an expression that became famous. He pointed his 44 Magnum pistol at one of the villains and said, "Go ahead, make my day!" In other words, he wanted a reason to shoot him. It did not have to be a good reason, just any reason, and he would have blown him away.

The heroes in the Bible are very different from Clint Eastwood's portrayal of Dirty Harry. These heroes in the Faith Hall of Fame were humble heroes. Hebrews 11 describes how they glorified God by their great deeds. Through faith they subdued kingdoms. They stopped the mouths of lions. Out of weakness they were made strong. They defeated armies and raised the dead. They were not afraid of death. Some of them died and suffered for their faith. They had an attitude that said, "You can kill me if you want to. I am not afraid of being stoned or being sawn in half. Go ahead, make my day!" The Bible goes on to say the world is not worthy of such great heroes.

God has Provided Something Better for Us

These heroes of faith did mighty things. However, their work will not be complete until we take God's promises and do mighty deeds. They have to wait for us to finish the work they started. We have to live a life of faith and bring glory to God so they will see the completion of their work.

> And these all, having obtained a good report through faith, received not the promise: God having provided some better thing for us, that they without us should not be made perfect.
>
> (Hebrews 11:39-40).

What was the promise they did not receive? God told Abraham that his children and his children's children would be a blessing to the world (Genesis 22:16-18). Abraham by faith knew that Jesus Christ would be one of his descendants (John 8:56). Abraham by faith saw there would be a day when Jesus would come to save the world. Years before Jesus was born Abraham saw Him coming by faith. Abraham and the other great men of faith in the Old Testament could not receive the promise of Jesus in their time. They had to see Jesus by faith.

Did you realize you know more about Jesus than the men in the Old Testament? You have a written record made by eyewitnesses in the New Testament to tell you who Jesus was and what He did. You also have wonderful letters to the early Christian churches. You have more information to work with than the people of the Old Testament do.

These ancient witnesses surround us. They are still alive in heaven. Someday we will meet them, and we will be able to say we completed what they had started. Because they have left us this tremendous testimony, we should desire to purify ourselves and run the race of faith that is before us.

Wherefore seeing we also are compassed about with so great a cloud of witnesses, let us lay aside every weight, and the sin which doth so easily beset us, and let us run with patience the race that is set before us, Looking unto Jesus the author and finisher of our faith; who for the joy that was set before him endured the cross, despising the shame, and is set down at the right hand of the throne of God.

(Hebrews 12:1-2).

The heroes of faith are waiting for us to glorify God in our lives and finish the work they started. We can do something they cannot. We can share the Good News of Jesus with a dying world. This is the privilege we have been given. We live in a time the ancient men could only dream about. We live in the time of the risen, all-powerful Savior who openly triumphed over the forces of evil.

YOU CAN TRIUMPH OVER THE LIMITS IN YOUR LIFE
* * *

Forget Your Past

Many people are limited by memories of past failures. Why do you want to dwell on the memories of your past? You should forget the past. Think on the things God has in front of you. Think about how you are made to triumph in Jesus. Think about the calling of God on your life. Think about the wonderful things Jesus Christ has done for you.

The Apostle Paul understood the importance of forgetting the past and looking forward to what God had called him to do. He said,

> Brethren, I count not myself to have appre-
> hended: but this one thing I do, forgetting those
> things which are behind, and reaching forth unto
> those things which are before, I press toward the
> mark for the prize of the high calling of God in
> Christ Jesus. (Philippians 3:13-14).

The Apostle Paul also had advice on how to take control of thoughts that were contrary to the will of God. He
said,

> Casting down imaginations, and every high
> thing that exalteth itself against the knowledge of
> God, and bringing into captivity every thought to
> the obedience of Christ; (2 Corinthians 10:5).

You can replace thoughts of failures with thoughts of
success. Why do you want to live your life thinking about
past failures? That just reinforces the chances you will fail.
Replace that old picture of defeat and failure with a new
picture of victory and success.

God wants you to know you can triumph over the
Goliaths in your life. You can fulfill your destiny. You can
be a victorious overcomer in this life. Jesus has done the
work. He has already defeated the enemy. All you have to
do is to join in the victory parade. You can take your place
by the other great heroes of faith and walk in victory and
triumph over the limits in your life.

Rejoice in Your Victory!

At the close of an intercessory prayer service at our
church one night, God moved on us in a powerful way.
We began to rejoice and shout. We were not being foolish
or crazy. We were just celebrating our victory in Jesus. We
were triumphing over the enemy.

During this time of rejoicing it became real to me that

there are no more limits as to what we can do in God. This means that whatever the situation is in your life, there are no more limits to hold you back. Wherever you are physically, spiritually, emotionally, or financially, there are no more limits in God. You can live with your discontentment, indebtedness, depression and distress, or you can become mighty in God.

You can and should live in triumph over the limits in your life. You can do nothing in yourself, but you can do all things through Christ that strengthens you. You have no excuse for failure. You can and should live a life of victory that brings glory to God!

In Christ, you are free from those things that are limiting you from being all you can be. There are no more limits. Enjoy your triumph in Christ. Rejoice in your victory!

WHAT ARE LIMITS?

LIMITS ARE BOUNDARIES

* * *

Prisons Without Walls

Years ago, when my wife Jeanne and I first started in the ministry, we would visit all kinds of prisons. One prison we visited was a federal prison in Michigan. I remember we spent the night there with the prisoners. We slept in bedrolls on the gymnasium floor, with just a net to separate us from the prisoners. This was a wonderful experience because we were able to talk to the prisoners one on one. Many of them were not Christians, and some of them wanted to find out about Christianity and change their lives.

The warden of this Michigan prison gave me some insight into how we form limits in our minds. He said prisons are institutions and, after being there for years, the prisoners become institutionalized. They have established limits within themselves. The warden told me something I will never forget. He said if they were to remove the fences, most of the guys would not want to leave. He said many of them had become so comfortable being in prison that it would be hard for them to think about living any other way.

35

The prison fence represents the boundary in their minds. It limits how far they can go. After spending years within their limits, the prisoners have grown accustomed to them. If the physical barrier were removed, the mental barrier would still be there. They have been conditioned to never go beyond that boundary. They have become imprisoned in their minds.

Limits are boundaries. Everyone has limits. Limits are a part of everyday life. Everyone has limiting circumstances and limiting ways of thinking. When Jesus comes into our lives, He wants to remove the limits that are hindering us. We, however, are so used to the status quo that we find it hard to venture beyond our limits. We are imprisoned in our minds.

Good Limits and Bad Limits

I want to make a distinction between good limits and bad limits. Good limits are limits that keep us from living foolishly and hurting ourselves and others. Bad limits are limits that keep us from experiencing God in our lives.

When I am talking about no more limits, I am not talking about disobeying laws and other limits that are necessary to keep our lives in order. I am not talking about living foolishly. I am not talking about going out and charging up all your credit cards or speeding recklessly down the highway.

When I am talking about no more limits, I am talking about limits in our lives that keep God at a distance. I am talking about limits we have accepted that are contrary to the will of God. These are bad limits and need to be removed.

Bad limits keep us from receiving the fullness of God.

These limits keep us from receiving healing for our bodies. These limits keep us from receiving wholeness in our souls and in our emotions. These limits keep us from entering into worship. These limits keep us from entering into Christian service and helping others.

We all should understand that we need to set good limits. We should understand we must exercise self-control over many things. The limits we need to eliminate are the limits that have kept God from fulfilling His purpose and plan for our lives. God wants us to live a life with no more limits that brings glory to Him and joy for us.

HOW ISRAEL LIMITED GOD

* * *

God Miraculously Delivered Israel Out of Egypt

The stories in the Bible are given for our instruction. The Bible talks about how God was limited by the nation of Israel in the wilderness. These limits grieved God.

> How oft did they provoke him in the wilderness, and grieve him in the desert! Yea, they turned back and tempted God, and limited the Holy One of Israel. (Psalms 78:40-41).

The Israelites had been slaves in Egypt for many years. God used Moses to deliver them and set them free. Many mighty miracles were performed, and the Egyptians were ruined with many plagues. Finally, the Pharaoh of Egypt agreed to let Moses take the Israelites away (Exodus 12:31).

At the last minute, Pharaoh changed his mind. He set out with his army to stop the Israelites from leaving Egypt. But God had a different plan. Moses parted the Red

Sea and the Israelites walked across on dry land. When the Pharaoh and his army tried to follow them, the sea covered them over and they all perished (Exodus 14:28). This was a tremendous triumph for the Israelites.

The Israelites rejoiced in their triumph over the enemy.

> **Then sang Moses and the children of Israel this song unto the LORD, and spake, saying, I will sing unto the LORD, for he hath triumphed gloriously: the horse and his rider hath he thrown into the sea.** (Exodus 15:1).

God continued to do great and mighty deeds for his people. God met their needs in the desert. God caused water to flow from rocks and food called manna to fall from heaven (Exodus 16:1-17:7). God gave them a pillar of fire at night to keep them warm and a cloud by day to keep them cool (Exodus 13:21-22). God demonstrated His willingness to meet every need they had. They experienced miracles every day in the desert.

Because of Unbelief They Died in the Wilderness

God moved the Israelites from Egypt. He delivered them from their enemies. Their needs were met in the desert. They lived in the presence of God. They were no longer slaves under harsh taskmasters. They were free. However, they did not act like they were free. Even though they had been given all manner of blessings, they continued to think like slaves. They had been physically liberated from slavery, but they continued to behave like slaves. They did not receive all the blessings God had intended for them. God took them out of Egypt, but God could not take Egypt out of them.

The Israelites that were slaves in Egypt never made it to the Promised Land. They rebelled against God many times. They wandered in the desert for 40 years until they all had died. God had intended for these ex-slaves to return as free people to the promised land, a land flowing with milk and honey, but their unbelief kept them from entering the promised land (Hebrews 3:17-19).

These ex-slaves never lived in the Promised Land. When they were on the border of the Promised Land, they saw heavily defended cities and giants in the land. They were full of doubt, fear and unbelief. They saw themselves as grasshoppers in comparison to the inhabitants. They rebelled against God and refused to take possession of their Promised Land (Numbers 13:1-14:45).

The Israelites forgot how God had drowned the mightiest army in the world, the Egyptian army, on their behalf. They forgot how God had caused them to triumph over their enemies. They refused to believe they could take the land. They failed to realize God was the One who was going to drive out the inhabitants of the land before them. All they had to do was obey and believe God, and they would have been allowed to live in their Promised Land.

Only two men had faith to believe they could have the Promised Land: Joshua and Caleb. Of all the slaves who left Egypt, they were the only two who were allowed into the Promised Land (Numbers 14:6, 24). These two men were full of faith, and they lived to conquer and triumph over their enemies. All the rest of the ex-slaves died in the desert.

It was left up to the children of the ex-slaves to possess the Promised Land. When the children of the ex-slaves grew up and their rebellious parents had died, then God allowed them to leave the wilderness and take the promised land (Joshua 5:2-7). They had to fight, but it was God who provided the victory. They went on to receive by faith and obedience the inheritance God had promised their parents.

Learning from Israel's Example of Unbelief

The following passage tells the people of Israel limited God while they were wandering in the desert. There are several things we can see from these Scriptures. They provoked God. They grieved God. They tempted God. They limited God. They forgot how He had miraculously saved them from slavery.

> How oft did they provoke him in the wilderness, and grieve him in the desert! Yea, they turned back and tempted God, and limited the Holy One of Israel. They remembered not his hand, nor the day when he delivered them from the enemy. How he had wrought his signs in Egypt, and his wonders in the field of Zoan:
>
> (Psalms 78:40-43).

> But with whom was he grieved forty years? was it not with them that had sinned, whose carcases fell in the wilderness? And to whom sware he that they should not enter into his rest, but to them that believed not? So we see that they could not enter in because of unbelief.
>
> (Hebrews 3:17-19).

Let us look more in depth at these verses to learn how the Israelites limited God. Let us learn from their example of unbelief and make the same mistakes they did and miss the blessings God has in store for us.

Israel Provoked God

Provoking God means they rebelled against God.

Rebellion is an evil thing to God. Rebellion is like the sin of witchcraft (1 Samuel 15:23). Rebellion is saying no when you should be saying yes. Rebellion is stubbornly going against God when He is trying to lead you forward.

God instructs us in many ways. He may use the Bible, or His Spirit or a person. He has many pastors, evangelists, prophets, teachers and apostles to help us. Whenever God tries to instruct you or counsel you, and you rebel against Him, you are provoking Him.

You demonstrate unbelief when you rebel against God. You are saying, in essence, that your way is better than God's way. You show that you do not trust God and His goodness. Rebellion is a lack of understanding and appreciation of God's true love and concern for you. Rebellion upsets God and limits God from blessing you.

Israel Grieved God

The Bible says the Israelites grieved God (Psalms 78:40, Hebrews 3:17). God is grieved when you do not believe His promises. You actually cause God sorrow when you do not believe He will make a way for you to receive His blessings. Unbelief causes you to limit God. He is pleased when you act in faith. He is grieved when you have unbelief. We cannot receive God's promises when we operate in unbelief. Unbelief causes God sorrow. The reverse of this is true. When we operate in faith, we bring joy to God.

Israel Turned Back

Because Israel did not believe God they turned back. The Bible says they limited God (Psalms 78:41). Anytime that you turn back from your forward motion, you limit God. He cannot help you when you turn back.

The Apostle Paul told the Galatians he was concerned for them because they turned back to bondage after they had known God. Jesus had come to them and shown them a new way to live. Instead of trusting in Jesus and moving forward in freedom, they turned back to dead elements of religious bondage.

> But now, after that ye have known God, or rather are known of God, how turn ye again to the weak and beggarly elements, whereunto ye desire again to be in bondage? Ye observe days, and months, and times, and years. I am afraid of you, lest I have bestowed upon you labour in vain.
>
> (Galatians 4:9-11)

Religious bondage is a product of man's desire to control people with religious legalism. God had set the Galatians free from religious legalism (Galatians 5:1), and yet they decided to turn back. Once you are free from those things that had you bound, turning back to them is never acceptable.

Jesus told the disciples that no man is fit for the kingdom of God when he puts his hand to the plow and then turns back (Luke 9:62). Another term for turning back is backsliding. You limit God when you backslide and return to a life of disobedience to God.

What lies ahead for the believer is much greater than anything that is left behind. One of the tricks of the devil is to convince you that your best days were in your past. The truth is that your best days lie ahead.

Israel Tempted God

Israel continually tried to tempt or test God (Psalms 78:41). They would not believe God when he spoke through Moses. They demanded God to prove himself over and over again. God does not have to prove himself.

Jesus withstood temptation. Jesus would not fall for the devil's tricks. Jesus did not allow Himself to tempt God. Jesus did not limit God like the Israelites by tempting God. Jesus was the perfect example of the unlimited potential of God.

> Then the devil taketh him up into the holy city, and setteth him on a pinnacle of the temple, And saith unto him, If thou be the Son of God, cast thyself down: for it is written, He shall give his angels charge concerning thee: and in their hands they shall bear thee up, lest at any time thou dash thy foot against a stone. Jesus said unto him, It is written again, Thou shalt not tempt the Lord thy God. (Matthew 4:5-7)

In this temptation the devil quotes Scripture to Jesus and asks Him to throw Himself down from the top of the temple to prove to everybody He is the Son of God. You tempt God when you misapply the Scriptures. The Scriptures were given to do the will of God, not the will of the devil or the will of man. Jesus came to do the will of God. He did not have to show off His powers to prove anything to the devil or anyone. Jesus was confident in who He was and the purpose God had for Him. He had faith in God and knew He needed to do only what His heavenly Father wanted Him to do. He only used His power to suit God's purposes and not the devil's.

We must believe by faith that God will do what He says He will do in His Word. We should not need miraculous signs from God to have faith in God. Jesus taught that an evil generation seeks miraculous signs (Matthew 12:39). Many people ask for miraculous signs to prove things. When you ask God for miraculous signs to help you believe, you are tempting God. Belief does not need miraculous signs. Unbelief needs miraculous signs. We must not tempt God with unbelief by asking for miraculous signs.

Miraculous signs should be a product of faith. We should have signs *following* our faith, not preceding it. When you reverse the order and require a sign first to believe, you are tempting God. Most people have it backwards. The proper order is to believe and then the miracles happen (Mark 16:17-18).

Israel Did Not Remember God

God performed many signs for Israel, and still they did not remember what He had done for them. They had forgotten how He miraculously delivered them from the Egyptians (Psalms 78:43-43).

Let us not forget what God has done for us! Do you remember when you were lost? Do you remember when you were ugly? Do you remember when church was the furthest thing from your mind? If you have been delivered from much, you ought to be grateful and thankful for much. You should remember and be thankful for all God has done for you.

When you forget where you were before Jesus was in your life, you limit God. You must remember what you were saved from and Who saved you. Remember Who brought you out of your lostness. Remember Who delivered you. Remember Who healed you. Remember what Jesus has already done for you.

Sometimes it is easy to forget what God has done in our lives. When we come across a little problem, a little trial, or a little obstacle, we soon forget what God has done for us.

Reminding ourselves of God's goodness and faithfulness in the past helps us to have faith in God for the present. We must realize God never changes (James 1:17). He is the same God He has always been (Hebrews 13:8). We are the ones who need to change.

Faith in God Releases You from Limits

By faith you have been set free from the limits and bondage of the devil. By faith you have been born again. By faith you have been made more than a conqueror through Jesus Christ. By faith you can do all things through Christ who strengthens you. Faith in God and His promises is the answer for unbelief. Faith in God releases you from the grip of unbelief and takes you into new territory. Faith in God allows you to receive from God all He has planned for you.

Unfortunately, many people never receive all God has planned for them. Not unlike the former Egyptian slaves, many of us fail to receive the blessings that God wants us to have. We fail to appropriate these blessings by faith, and we fail to partake of the best God has for us because of unbelief.

The Israelites who died in the wilderness limited God. It was not God's intention for them to die in the wilderness. He wanted them to believe and trust in Him. He wanted them to enter the Promised Land. They rebelled against God and they died in the wilderness. We need to consider these things and avoid being left in our own wilderness. Their example is given to us so we can have faith in God and not limit God with unbelief. Walking in faith is the remedy for unbelief. Walking in faith releases you from limits and helps you enter into the Promised Land of unlimited potential.

OVERCOMING THE LIMITS OF RELIGIOUS TRADITION

GOD DOES NOT TEST HIS CHILDREN WITH EVIL

* * *

God is Not Your Problem

I received a letter from a woman who was confused by a TV preacher who said God puts sickness and disease on people to teach them lessons. She had thought that God wanted her to be healthy. This preacher had put doubt in her mind when he said, "God uses the devil to teach His children lessons."

This woman could not understand why God would want the devil to make her sick. If He was using the devil, what was she supposed to be learning? She was sick and tired of being sick and tired. She wanted to know if I thought God sent the devil to teach her something, and if I thought God might not want her healed.

I knew I had to be careful how I answered. This woman was bedfast. She was at risk of dying at an early age. If I did not answer her carefully, I knew her life might be at stake. She had believed God for her healing, and now she was being taught that He had brought the problem on her to teach her something.

What Does the Bible Say About Evil?

I told this woman, "Since you asked me, let's look at what the Word says. You have to look at the whole Bible to understand what God is doing, and God does not use evil to tempt His children."

I told this woman to read James 1:13-17. These Scriptures plainly say God does not use evil to accomplish his purposes. I told her, "God did not send the devil to teach you a lesson. God wants to heal you."

> Let no man say when he is tempted, I am tempted of God: for God cannot be tempted with evil, neither tempteth he any man
>
> (James 1:13).

Another word for tempting is testing. God is not tested by evil and He does not test anyone with evil circumstances. This goes against His nature.

I have seen many sick people who are in bad shape from cancer and other illnesses. Sickness and disease is an evil thing. Anybody who says sickness and disease is something good has never spent time in the hospital praying for sick people. Sickness and disease kills people and destroys lives. Sickness and disease is evil. God does not use evil to test His children.

I have a difficult time believing God wants anyone to be sick. Jesus came to show us how to have abundant life (John 10:10). Abundant life must include health. I believe sickness and disease is a limit from which Jesus can set us free.

Jesus Carried Your Sicknesses and Pains

Healing has been controversial among churches for a long time. Many people do not believe healing is for today.

48

This is one subject to which I have given much thought. I believe many people are limiting God in the area of healing because of their religious tradition. Many will gladly teach spiritual healing is for today, but they will stop short of saying physical healing is for today.

I believe it is just as much the will of God to heal you physically as it is to heal you spiritually. Jesus' death on the cross paid the price for the redemption of humanity from sin. Jesus' death settled the sin issue and made a way for us to receive access to the favor of God. I believe physical healing is part of the plan of redemption.

I believe when you deny that physical healing is part of your redemption you are limiting God. When you deny that physical healing is part of redemption, you are not properly discerning the Lord's body and blood which was shed for you. Jesus' death on the cross was physical.

The communion we take as Christians is symbolic of the blood and body of Jesus. Paul said many believers did not properly discern the body of Christ that was broken for them and they became sick and died.

> But let a man examine himself, and so let him eat of that bread, and drink of that cup. For he that eateth and drinketh unworthily, eateth and drinketh damnation to himself, not discerning the Lord's body. For this cause many are weak and sickly among you, and many sleep.
>
> (1 Corinthians 11:28-30).

The Apostle Peter mentions healing along with forgiveness of sins. The Apostle Peter says the broken body of Jesus was for our healing. The Apostle Peter mentions the bloody marks Jesus had from being whipped were proof for healing.

> Who his own self bare our sins in his own
> body on the tree, that we, being dead to sins,
> should live unto righteousness: by whose stripes
> ye were healed.   (1 Peter 2:24).

This quotation from the Apostle Peter was based upon a Scripture in Isaiah. Isaiah gives us a picture of the suffering Jesus on the cross.

> Surely he hath borne our griefs, and carried
> our sorrows: yet we did esteem him stricken, smitten of God, and afflicted. But he was wounded for
> our transgressions, he was bruised for our iniquities: the chastisement of our peace was upon him;
> and with his stripes we are healed. (Isaiah 53:4-5).

It is interesting to notice the tense Isaiah used for healing. Isaiah used the present tense. He said, "with his stripes we are healed." Isaiah was looking *forward* prophetically to Jesus death. In 1 Peter 2:24, Peter uses the past tense of the same verb when he said, "by whose stripes you were healed." The Apostle Peter was looking *back* to the cross. **The death of Jesus on the cross was the focal point of the Bible.** Everything in the Bible points to the moment when humanity was redeemed from sin, sickness, disease, poverty and death.

The Prophet Isaiah says Jesus bore our griefs and carried our sorrows. The Hebrew word for "griefs" is the word "choliy" pronounced "khol-ee '." This word is translated as *grief* four times, but in other places this same word is translated *sickness* (twelve times) and *disease* (seven times). The word for "sorrows" is the Hebrew word "makob" pronounced "mak-obe'." This same word is also translated as *pain* in a couple of other places. This word can mean physical and mental pain.

When Isaiah says he "hath borne our griefs, and carried our sorrows," it would not be inappropriate to read, "Jesus bore our sicknesses, our diseases, our mental and our physical pains." When He died on the cross Jesus bore our sicknesses and carried our pains. Personalize this and repeat it to yourself. Say, "Jesus bore my sicknesses and carried my pains."

I can think of one other good example that shows Jesus died on the cross for our healing. When talking about His death on the cross, Jesus reminded His followers of the time the Israelites put a snake on a pole and were physically healed. Here's what happened: While they were wandering in the desert, they began complaining about their food and water. Thousands of snakes began to attack them in the desert, and many of them were dying from snakebites. God told Moses to make a brass serpent and put it upon a pole. When the Israelites were snakebitten, they could look at the serpent on the pole and live (Numbers 21:4-9).

This serpent on the pole was symbolic for Jesus on the cross. Jesus even said He was like the serpent in the wilderness:

> And as Moses lifted up the serpent in the wilderness, even so must the Son of man be lifted up: That whosoever believeth in him should not perish, but have eternal life. For God so loved the world, that he gave his only begotten Son, that whosoever believeth in him should not perish, but have everlasting life. For God sent not his Son into the world to condemn the world; but that the world through him might be saved. (John 3:14-17).

Healing is part of redemption. Jesus who knew no sin was made to be sin so that we might have righteousness

51

(2 Corinthians 5:21). Our righteousness in Christ entitles us to live forever and to have healing for the present.

Seek Healing When You Need It

The Bible tells us to seek help when we are sick. People who teach healing is not for today must have to go to great lengths to explain away the following Scripture:

> Is any sick among you? let him call for the elders of the church; and let them pray over him, anointing him with oil in the name of the Lord: And the prayer of faith shall save the sick, and the Lord shall raise him up; and if he have committed sins, they shall be forgiven him. (James 5:14-15).

Instead of making a tradition against healing, we should have traditions in our churches for healing. The early tradition was to have the elders of the church anoint with oil and pray for the sick. When the sick were prayed for they were healed. If they had sinned they were forgiven at the same time.

If God wanted some people to be sick, why would the Apostle James write this statement? He said if there be "any sick" among you, God will heal him if he is anointed with oil and prayed for in faith.

It seems as if the Apostle James expected all the sick people in the church to be healed. He did not question "if it be God's will." He did not say to let people stay sick a little longer to learn a lesson. He said the prayer of faith would save the sick. It is always God's will to heal those who come before the church and petition healing.

Jesus Demonstrated God's Will Concerning Healing

God the Father sent Jesus His Son to demonstrate love to the world. Jesus was God's love in action. Jesus said if you were looking at Him you would be looking at the Father (John 14:9). Jesus came and, with many signs and wonders, demonstrated God's willingness and ability to heal.

The Bible records no instance where Jesus sent someone away until they had suffered more and learned their lesson. The Bible clearly records Jesus doing many mighty healing miracles. He had power over all sicknesses and diseases.

> **And Jesus went about all the cities and villages, teaching in their synagogues, and preaching the gospel of the kingdom, and healing every sickness and every disease among the people. (Matthew 9:35).**

This verse does not say He healed just a few every now and then. It says He healed every sickness and every disease. Jesus demonstrated He was a healing savior. There were no limits on Jesus' willingness and ability to heal.

When Jesus was being arrested and taken away to be crucified, Peter used his sword to cut off an ear of one of the men who was arresting Jesus. Even then, when being led away to die, Jesus healed the man's ear (Luke 22:50-51).

I find it hard to imagine Jesus doing anything other than healing people. To say Jesus puts sickness on people to teach them something goes against everything you read about Him in the Bible. You have to base this type of thinking on religious traditions that deny the ability of God to work in our lives today.

OVERCOMING THE LIMITS OF RELIGIOUS TRADITION

* * *

Good and Bad Traditions

Not all traditions are bad. The traditions of baptisms

and of communion are good. These traditions are clearly outlined in the Bible. The traditions that are bad are religious traditions that hinder the power of God in the lives of people.

When someone says healing is not for today, or it might not be God's will to heal you now, these are bad traditions. If people are taught not to expect God to heal or bless them, they are being taught things which can limit God from working in their lives. In the case of healing, it is literally a matter of life and death. Rotten tradition can rob people from the lifesaving, healing power of God.

Many worthless traditions come from misunderstanding the nature and character of God. God is always good. God is not the source of your problems. God is always the answer to your problems. Sin, sickness, disease, poverty and death are all problems that exist in this fallen world. Jesus overcame all these problems. Jesus pointed out He was the source for abundant life. He contrasted His purpose to the purpose of the devil when He said,

> The thief cometh not, but for to steal, and to kill, and to destroy: I am come that they might have life, and that they might have it more abundantly. (John 10:10).

There is a spiritual outlaw in the earth. There is a real devil that causes real big problems. Jesus identified the devil as the source of crime and destruction. Jesus said the devil comes to kill, steal and destroy.

Many people who are caught up in bad religious traditions totally ignore the devil. They say all good and evil comes from God. Tradition teaches that the devil is just a tool used by God to beat His children into submission. Hurricanes, floods, tornadoes, your father-in-law dying of brain cancer...well, these are all acts of God. Insurance companies claim this, and many religious people believe and agree with this.

Traditions, which see evil circumstances originating from God, are worthless because they do not cause people to have faith toward God. They teach people to fear God for the wrong reasons. We should have a reverence and respect for God, but we should not be afraid to ask Him for help when we need it. God does not want us to base our religion on fear. He wants us to base our religion on faith. It pleases God when we have faith. Unbelief and fear impose limits upon Him.

Traditions that are not based upon faith but upon fear will always impose limits on people. God does not want you to be limited by fear. God wants you to be able to approach Him and to receive the good things you need for your life. You always need to approach God with the attitude that He is good, and He wants to bless you with good things.

> If ye then, being evil, know how to give good gifts unto your children, how much more shall your Father which is in heaven give good things to them that ask him? (Matthew 7:11).

Your Heavenly Father is a loving Father. God is not a child abuser. God is not a criminal. If God was put on trial and convicted of all the crimes He was accused of doing to His children, He would be sentenced to millions of years of jail time! However, this is a terrible misconception about God. God is good and not evil.

Your heavenly Father wants to provide good things to you as His child. God does not want you to be deprived of the things you need. God has many gifts He wants to give you as His child. If human parents desire only the best for their children, God's desire is even stronger to provide the best for His children.

Worthless Traditions Limit God

Jesus had spiritual power. The religious leaders in his day did not have spiritual power. They were limited. Jesus was unlimited.

Jesus demonstrated his power with many signs and wonders. He was able to demonstrate by example how God was willing to help people in their time of need. Jesus showed us the will of God. Jesus showed us what it was like to live without limits. He demonstrated there were no financial limits, no physical limits, no emotional limits and no spiritual limits that could not be overcome by the power of God.

Jesus had power to demonstrate the abundance of God over financial lack. He turned water into wine when the wine ran out at a wedding. (John 2:1-11). Jesus blessed a struggling fishing business with so many fish their nets broke (Luke 5:1-11). Jesus turned the limited resources of a few loaves and fishes into an unlimited supply of food to feed a multitude (Mark 15:15-21). Jesus even found creative ways to satisfy the tax collector. He sent Peter fishing and the first fish he caught had a gold coin in its mouth, which was enough to pay Peter's and His taxes (Matthew 17:24-27).

Jesus demonstrated the provision of God for healing and deliverance. There was no sickness or disease that could prevail over his authority. He healed and delivered sick children from the oppression of the devil (John 4:46-54, Mark 7:24-30, Mark 9:14-29). Jesus opened blind eyes and healed lame limbs (Matthew 9:27-31, John 9:1-41, Mark 3:1-6, Luke 13:10-17). Jesus raised those who had died before their time on several occasions (Luke 7:11-16, Matthew 9:18-26, John 11:1-45).

Jesus was an example of a man operating by the power of God to overcome all limiting situations. Jesus is the example for us to follow. He came to show us how to live our lives to give glory to God.

Jesus offered real solutions to the needs of people through the power of the Holy Spirit. The religious leaders offered no solutions through their man-made traditions. Their religion was shallow and powerless. Jesus' religion was deep and powerful, and overcame all the limits of religious tradition. Jesus was a bright light shining in the darkness. Worthless religious traditions are dark and void of any real solutions to life's problems.

Jesus scolded the religious leaders for taking the power out of the word of God through their worthless traditions.

> Making the word of God of none effect through your tradition, which ye have delivered: and many such like things do ye. (Mark 7:13).

Worthless traditions often act as limits in areas where the promises of God are concerned. If God promises something in the Bible, it should never be a question if it is God's will or not. If God promises something, it is available to all who believe. This applies to salvation, healing, prosperity or whatever you need. If there is a promise in the Bible, and you have faith to believe it applies to you, then you can receive what you need from God.

If you have been acting upon worthless traditions of

men, you have limited the power of God in your life.
Many people have been taught religiously week after week
that God brings sickness and disease, or that God takes
babies to heaven because he needs them there to brighten
heaven. People have been taught healing is not for today,
the time for miracles has passed, and God does not work
the same way he did in the Gospels and in the book of
Acts.

Traditions not based upon sound knowledge and
understanding of the will of God and the Word of God act
as limits in many people's lives. These traditions become
limits or boundaries, which prevent people from experiencing the goodness and mercy of God. These limits must
be broken before people can receive all God has for them.

The Truth Will Free You From the Limits of
Religious Tradition

Jesus said if you continue to study the Word and apply
the Word of God in your life, you will begin to know
truth, and truth will set you free. The truth about God is
what will set you free from religious and traditional limits
that are based upon wrong conceptions and wrong beliefs
about God.

> **Then said Jesus to those Jews which believed**
> **on him, If ye continue in my word, then are ye my**
> **disciples indeed; And ye shall know the truth, and**
> **the truth shall make you free.**   (John 8:31-32).

Another passage in the book of James talks about the
same thing. If you are a doer of the Word of God, and if
you continue to obey the truth of the Word, then you will
be blessed.

> But be ye doers of the word, and not hearers
> only, deceiving your own selves. For if any be a
> hearer of the word, and not a doer, he is like unto
> a man beholding his natural face in a glass: For he
> beholdeth himself, and goeth his way, and straight-
> way forgetteth what manner of man he was. But
> whoso looketh into the perfect law of liberty, and
> continueth therein, he being not a forgetful hearer,
> but a doer of the work, this man shall be blessed
> in his deed. (James 1:22-25).

Perfect Law of liberty

James calls the Word of God the "perfect law of liberty." The word of God will set you free from the limits
imposed upon you by worthless religious traditions.

Do Not Settle for the Limits of Religious Traditions

Many man-made traditions are based upon wrong
beliefs. These traditions teach you to settle for the tradition
instead of believing for the fullness and richness of God.
People who are more than conquerors and triumphant in
Christ should never settle for the compromise of worthless
traditions. Reject the limits of man-made traditions that
keep God from operating in your life. Receive the fullness
of God and His richness in every area of your life. Do not
settle for the hollow and empty commandments of men.
These are poor substitutes from the freedom found in a true
relationship with a living and loving God.

Pride and arrogance lead men to give man-made traditions and doctrines a high place in their life. Jesus said
these works were a vain attempt at worshipping God.

Howbeit in vain do they worship me, teaching for
doctrines the commandments of men. And he said unto
them, Full well ye reject the commandment of God, that
ye may keep your own tradition. (Mark 7:7,9).

Today, many religious men have a higher regard for their own vain traditions than they do for the Word of God. Their lives are devoid of the power of God and they teach others to be like themselves. Vain traditions strangle the Word of God. Vain traditions explain away the power behind the miracles of God. Vain traditions rob people from receiving their blessings from God. Vain traditions rob people from expecting miracles to happen. Vain traditions interfere with true worship and fellowship with God.

Jesus Triumphed Over the Limits of Religious Traditions

Jesus had compassion on sinners. He gently led sinners to see the truth. He came to show us that everyone is a sinner. Only through Him can we find salvation. Only through following Him and obeying His words, can we live a life free from the limits of religious tradition.

On the other hand, Jesus had wrath and anger toward the religious hypocrites. He was quite outspoken against the established religious leaders of his day. He openly rebuked them, calling them "white-washed tombs full of deadness and uncleanness" (Matthew 23:270. Jesus exposed the powerlessness of religious tradition. Religious hypocrites hated Jesus. They plotted to kill Him and hinder His work. Eventually, they put Jesus on trial and brought about His death on the cross. However, Jesus triumphed over the religious leaders of His day. After they had Him crucified, they thought it was over. They were wrong. Jesus rose from the dead and their troubles were multiplied. Jesus sent forth His disciples in His name throughout the world with the message of hope and salvation. Jesus' resurrection was the ultimate triumph over the limits of dead religion and useless traditions!

UNDERSTANDING LIMITING CIRCUMSTANCES

LEARNING ABOUT LIMITS FROM THE LIFE OF JOB

* * *

Job is a Story About Triumphing Over Limits

The book of Job in the Old Testament describes a man who experienced great suffering. He faced and overcame severe hardships. He was a wealthy family man and lost almost everything he valued. He lost his children. He lost his financial security, and he lost his health. The story of Job describes his struggles and his attempts to understand his sufferings. Job faced tremendous hardships, but he also triumphed over his circumstances. In the end Job was restored by God. Job received back his physical health, prosperity, and family.

Many people emphasize the sufferings of Job. The emphasis should not be on the suffering of Job, but on his victory and triumph over his limiting circumstances. He overcame his limiting circumstances with the help of God. Job is a wonderful story of a man's triumph over limiting circumstances by the grace of God.

Job was a Good Man

Many people think bad things do not happen to good

people. Life is not always fair. Many times bad things do happen to good people. Job was the best man on the earth during his day. Listen to what God said about Job:

> And the LORD said unto Satan, Hast thou considered my servant Job, that there is none like him in the earth, a perfect and an upright man, one that feareth God, and escheweth evil?   (Job 1:8).

God gave Job a great character reference. He said he was an upright man and reverenced God and hated evil. God was not angry at Job. God thought Job was a good man.

Job had a Spiritual Enemy

Unfortunately, Job does not know he has an accuser working against him. Satan was accusing him before God. The devil came to kill, steal and destroy. The devil opposes everything good. Job could not see the spiritual enemy who was about to attack him.

The devil accused Job before God (Job 1:9-11). God acknowledged the devil's right to steal, kill and destroy. However, God never changed his faithful confession about Job:

> And the LORD said unto Satan, Behold, all that he hath is in thy power; only upon himself put not forth thine hand. So Satan went forth from the presence of the LORD.   (Job 1:12).

After Satan leaves God, Job finds himself in the middle of tremendous turmoil. Raiders come and steal his oxen, donkeys and camels. Raiders kill his servants. A lightning storm kills all his sheep. His sons and daughters are having a party and a tornado kills them all (Job 1:13-19).

Job Wrongly Blamed God for His Problems

Job did not know Satan had the power to attack him.

Job could not read the book of Job and see behind the scenes. He thought God was the source of his distress. Job did not understand the devil was the force behind death and destruction.

Job did not know any better so he blames God for his problems. After he had suffered great loss, the following Bible verses describe his reaction.

> Then Job arose, and rent his mantle, and shaved his head, and fell down upon the ground, and worshipped, And said, Naked came I out of my mother's womb, and naked shall I return thither: the LORD gave, and the LORD hath taken away; blessed be the name of the LORD. In all this Job sinned not, nor charged God foolishly.
>
> (Job 1:20-22).

Although Job thought God took his family and wealth from him, this was not true. The death and destruction were the result of Satan's attacks against him.

Notice this verse said Job had not sinned or charged God foolishly. Job was not held accountable for not knowing who it was that came to steal, kill and destroy. Job thought it was God because he did not know any better.

Job's problems became even worse. After he lost his children, servants and possessions, the devil once again accused Job before God. Job had painful sores from his head to his toes (Job 2:1-8). His wife even wanted him to die. Look at what she said to him:

> Then said his wife unto him, Dost thou still retain thine integrity? curse God, and die. But he said unto her, Thou speakest as one of the foolish women speaketh. What? shall we receive good at the hand of God, and shall we not receive evil? In all this did not Job sin with his lips. (Job 2:9-10).

Again, Job's statements were untrue concerning God. (Read James 1:13,17.) Job entered into a time of deep despair. His friends came and tried to help him, but his friends did not know any more about the cause of his problems than he did.

Job's Friends Wrongfully Condemned Him

Job's friends believed Job had committed some terrible sin and was being punished by God. This was not true. God was pleased with Job. God was not angry at him. Job's friends tried to convince Job his sufferings were brought about because of his wickedness Job 2:11-32:1). This could not have been further from the truth. Job was a great example of a decent human being.

Job's friends never won their case against Job. God eventually rebuked Job's friends for not speaking correctly.

> And it was so, that after the LORD had spoken these words unto Job, the LORD said to Eliphaz the Temanite, My wrath is kindled against thee, and against thy two friends: for ye have not spoken of me the thing that is right, as my servant Job hath. (Job 42:7).

God instructed them to make an offering to God and to ask Job to pray for them. When Job prayed for them, God forgave them of their sins.

> Therefore take unto you now seven bullocks and seven rams, and go to my servant Job, and offer up for yourselves a burnt offering; and my servant Job shall pray for you: for him will I accept: lest I deal with you after your folly, in that ye have not spoken of me the thing which is right, like my servant Job. So Eliphaz the Temanite and Bildad the Shuhite and Zophar the Naamathite went, and did according as the LORD commanded them: the LORD also accepted Job. (Job 42:8-9).

God does not punish people for their sins by inflicting them with sickness and poverty. God does not punish people by killing their loved ones. When Job's friends claimed God was punishing Job with disease, poverty, and the death of his children and servants, God became angry at them.

God is not pleased when we attribute death, disease and destruction to him. God is good and not evil. Job's friends did not correctly perceive the source of Job's problems, and God would not accept them until they made an offering and Job prayed for them.

JOB TRIUMPHED OVER HIS LIMITS

* * *

Job Needed Faith and Grace

Job was one of the finest men ever born. If Job was not suffering because of his sinful actions, what was Job's problem?

Job had two big problems. Job did not operate in faith concerning his family and business, and Job thought he was righteous because of his good deeds. Job did not have great faith at this point in his life. He had great fear. He was in despair and admitted what happened to him was something he greatly feared.

> For the thing which I greatly feared is come
> upon me, and that which I was afraid of is come
> unto me.   (Job 3:25).

Fear does not overcome the world, and in the absence of faith, great fear brings defeat. Job needed to overcome his fear and obtain faith to receive victory over the adverse circumstances in his life.

Job's other big problem was that he thought he could

be made righteous by his good deeds. Job did not understand that no person, no matter how perfect, can be righteous by earning points for doing good. Everyone must be made righteous by God's provision alone. God gives righteousness to everyone as a free gift. Salvation comes by the grace of God and is received by faith (Ephesians 2:8).

Job needed faith and grace to overcome his terrible circumstances. Job could not overcome his problems without the help of God. Job needed to hear from God to find the faith and grace he needed to overcome his limits.

God Speaks to Job

God never abandoned Job and God was not the cause of Job's sufferings. God was the answer to his troubles. God knew Job was in trouble because God hears the cries of those who are suffering (Psalms 34:17). Job needed to have faith in God. The Apostle Paul in the book of Romans talks about how faith for salvation comes from hearing the voice of God.

> **For whosoever shall call upon the name of the Lord shall be saved. How then shall they call on him in whom they have not believed? and how shall they believe in him of whom they have not heard? and how shall they hear without a preacher?... So then faith cometh by hearing, and hearing by the word of God.   (Romans 10:13-17).**

Faith comes by hearing the Word of God. Job needed to hear God's voice to be saved from his terrible circumstances. God speaks to him from the middle of a mighty whirlwind.

> **Then the LORD answered Job out of the whirlwind, and said, Who is this that darkeneth counsel by words without knowledge? Gird up**

now thy loins like a man; for I will demand of thee,
and answer thou me.   (Job 38:1-3).

God does not have to answer Job's accusations against Him. God said Job did not know what he was talking about. Job tried to blame God for his circumstances, but it was not God who was accusing him and tempting him.

Job has to answer a series of questions God asks him. Through these questions God begins to reveal his character and nature to Job. This builds Job's faith. God begins to lead Job out of the depths of despair by focusing Job's attention on Him and not on his troubles.

God asked Job questions which made him realize His magnificence. His questions dealt with the wonders of creation. Who made the earth? Who made the boundaries of the oceans? Who made snow and hail? Who feeds lions and ravens? Who makes horses strong and eagles to nest on mountaintops? (Job 38:4-39:30).

God wanted Job to realize he is not to accuse God of doing anything evil to him. God continued to ask Job questions.

> Gird up thy loins now like a man: I will demand of thee, and declare thou unto me. Wilt thou also disannul my judgment? wilt thou condemn me, that thou mayest be righteous?
>
> (Job 40:7-8).

God pointed out a fatal flaw in Job's thinking. Job thought his good deeds made him righteous before God. Job thought he should not have to suffer because of his good works. He failed to realize he could only be justified by faith and not works.

Job had to accept his righteousness through God by faith. Job could not save himself. Job had to accept the fact he was not righteous because of his deeds. He was only righteous by faith in God.

Jesus is the only One who was completely righteous. By recognizing our need for a Savior, we accept God's provision for righteousness. Our righteousness comes only by faith in Jesus Christ (Romans 3:22). Just like Job, we cannot be made righteous by our own works.

God continued to reveal more about Himself to Job. This progressive revelation brought Job to a point of greater faith and trust in God. He overwhelmed Job with His greatness (Job 40:9-41:34). Job took his eyes off his terrible situation, and put his eyes on the wonders and the glory of God. When Job shifted his focus from seeing his problems to seeing the wonders of the Creator, he realized his mistake. Job recognized God is not the cause of his problems. He saw God in a positive light.

Through his conversation with God, Job received faith from the Word of God. God's Word and instruction to Job took him from a place of great fear to a place of faith in God. His faith in God is what helped him make the necessary changes in his life to have victory over his circumstances.

Job Realized He Was Wrong

Job's personal interaction with his Creator broke the limits in his life and brought him to a place of repentance. When Job saw the goodness of God and compared it to his own goodness, he saw how inadequate he was.

Listen to what Job said as he realized he had falsely blamed God for his problems:

> Then Job answered the LORD, and said, I know that thou canst do every thing, and that no thought can be withholden from thee. Who is he that hideth counsel without knowledge? therefore

have I uttered that I understood not; things too
wonderful for me, which I knew not. Hear, I
beseech thee, and I will speak: I will demand of
thee, and declare thou unto me. I have heard of
thee by the hearing of the ear: but now mine eye
seeth thee. Wherefore I abhor myself, and repent
in dust and ashes.   (Job 42:1-6).

He now understands the goodness of God. He saw
how he needed to completely put his trust in God's plan
and purpose for his life.

Job repented from his self-righteousness. He accepted
the grace of God and was restored. Job's restoration was
not just a spiritual restoration. Job's restoration included
his health, his prosperity and his peace of mind.

Job Triumphed Over the Power of the Devil

Job is a good example of a man who, with God's help,
triumphed over his limits. Faith in God brought him salvation and deliverance from his circumstances and caused
him to triumph over the power of the devil.

Job's triumph over his suffering came when he had a
better understanding of the goodness and the grace of
God. Job gained a deeper understanding of the nature of
God and developed a triumphant faith in the power of
God to deliver and heal him. Job gave the world a wonderful example of God's willingness and ability to redeem
and alleviate the suffering of man from poverty, disease,
sorrow and despair.

So the LORD blessed the latter end of Job
more than his beginning: for he had fourteen thousand sheep, and six thousand camels, and a thousand yoke of oxen, and a thousand she asses. He

had also seven sons and three daughters. And he called the name of the first, Jemima; and the name of the second, Kezia; and the name of the third, Kerenhappuch. And in all the land were no women found so fair as the daughters of Job: and their father gave them inheritance among their brethren. After this lived Job an hundred and forty years, and saw his sons, and his sons' sons, even four generations. So Job died, being old and full of days. (Job 42:12-17).

You Can Triumph Over Your Circumstances

The story of Job ends in a great triumph. God restored everything the devil took from Job. God saved Job from all his troubles. God caused Job to triumph over sickness, poverty, sorrow and despair. God restored his riches, his health and his family. Job is an example of how God wants to bless His people.

Jesus came to destroy the works of the devil. Jesus wants you to triumph over the limiting circumstances in your life. You can triumph over sickness, poverty, sorrow and despair. Jesus can help you be triumphant over every attack of the devil. There are no more limits that can stand against you.

You can hear the voice of God. You can read God's precious promises in the Bible. You can have a victorious faith that overcomes the limits of the world. No matter how terrible your circumstances, and no matter how bad you have been attacked by the devil, there are no limits that God cannot help you overcome. Faith and grace can enable you to triumph over all your circumstances like Job triumphed over his.

CONQUERING LIMITING CIRCUMSTANCES

UNDERSTANDING THE WILL OF GOD

* * *

All Things Do Not Always Work Out for Good

One of the tactics of the enemy is to get you to blame God for all your problems. The devil makes people think God is working to destroy their lives, when in reality he is the one responsible. The book of Job clearly shows it was the devil that came to kill Job's children and servants. It was the devil who caused men to steal all his valuable livestock. It was the devil who afflicted Job's body with painful sores. The devil was working behind the scenes to bring ruin and destruction into the life of Job.

Many Christians do not understand why things happen the way they do. They just go from one bad circumstance into another. They are blind to the spiritual nature of things. The devil, the god of this world, has deceived them. Many of them do not recognize his deceitfulness. They go through life without understanding the subtle (and sometimes not so subtle) limits they accept in their lives. These limits have their origin in darkness and are the result of the enemy's craftiness and deception. Many people think everything that happens to them is from God. They are blind to the spiritual reality and are limited by their lack of knowledge.

71

Some people try to find the good in their circumstances. They have been told "all things work together for good," but they are not sure what this means. This is a partial quote from Romans 8:38. This partial quotation is used as a blanket statement to cover any problems they may come across. This is another one of those religious traditions that does more harm than good.

If a tree falls on their house, they say, "Well, you know, all things work together for good." If they have a car wreck, they say, "Well, you know, all things work together for good." If their brother-in-law dies of cancer, they say, "Well, you know, all things work together for good."

These people have been told all these things work together for good, but they are not sure how all these things work together for good. These people fail to take into consideration that they have a spiritual enemy who is trying to ruin their lives and they are blind to his evil schemes at work in their lives.

All things do not always work out for the good. A person dying and going to hell is not good. A baby starving and dying of malnutrition is not good. Wars that kill millions of people are not good. Drunk drivers killing people is not good. Floods, hurricanes and famines are not good. Sin, sickness, poverty and disease are not good. These things have their origin from the devil.

What Does All Things Working Together for Good Really Mean?

If everything that happens is not good, what does "all things work together for good" really mean? To better understand this, let us look at Romans 8 where this is written:

And we know that all things work together for good to them that love God, to them who are the called according to his purpose. (Romans 8:28)

There is a lot more to this verse than *all things work together for good*. The rest of the verse gives us valuable insight into what this really means. It says, *to them that love God, to them who are the called according to his purpose.*

This verse is telling you that all things work together for good when the proper conditions are met. The conditions are you have to love God and you have to be obedient to His calling for your life. If you are not in love with God, and if you are not being obedient to God and serving Him according to His purpose for your life, you cannot say "all things work together for good."

It is vitally important that you understand what the will of God is for your life. The Bible is given to you to instruct you in the ways of God. God has a plan and a purpose for your life. He has predestinated you to be conformed to the image of His Son Jesus.

Not all the circumstances you come across are God's will for your life. You will have problems in life. You will face battles everyday. There are spiritual forces at work behind the scenes that shape your circumstances. You live in a fallen world that is in darkness. The darkness causes suffering and hardships. Trials and tribulations are an inevitable part of life you must deal with.

Your Faith in God's Word will be Tried

The Word of God is like a seed in your heart. Your heart is a field where the Word is sown. Some seeds never grow, and some seeds do grow and produce a harvest. Jesus tells us that God's Word will be tested by adverse circumstances. God's Word in your heart is what the devil comes to steal because he wants to keep you from receiving your blessings from God.

> The sower soweth the word. And these are they by the way side, where the word is sown; but when they have heard, Satan cometh immediately, and taketh away the word that was sown in their hearts. (Mark 4:14-15)

The devil does not want God to be glorified through your faith in God's Word. If you do not produce a harvest from God's Word, the devil will beat you up. You will have to settle for sickness, disease and poverty. You will have to accept defeat. The devil wants you to become mad at God and stop believing God's word is true.

> And these are they likewise which are sown on stony ground; who, when they have heard the word, immediately receive it with gladness; And have no root in themselves, and so endure but for a time: afterward, when affliction or persecution ariseth for the word's sake, immediately they are offended. (Mark 4:16-17)

Your faith in God's Word will be tried. Trouble comes to discourage you and to try to deceive you into believing God's Word is not working. The devil wants to destroy your faith in God's Word. You can fail at this point, or you can continue to believe God's Word is true and receive your harvest.

You should also expect your faith to stand. Your faith is based upon the completed work of Jesus Christ. Jesus Christ strengthens you in your weakness and will always cause you to triumph over your tests and trials.

> My brethren, count it all joy when ye fall into
> divers temptations; Knowing this, that the trying
> of your faith worketh patience. But let patience
> have her perfect work, that ye may be perfect and
> entire, wanting nothing. (James 1:2-4)

Suffering for the Wrong Reasons

There are two aspects of suffering I need to explain.
There is suffering for doing good and there is suffering as
a result of not obeying God or not believing God's Word is
true. This second type of bad suffering is avoidable.

In Chapter 3 we talked about the how the Israelites
who left Egypt could not enter into their Promised Land
because they disobeyed God. Their children entered in,
but they could not enter in because of their unbelief. They
lost the right to live in the Promised Land because of fear,
doubt, unbelief and rebellion against God. They would
not have had to suffer living in a desert wilderness if they
had been obedient to God.

You can suffer as a Christian for doing good, or you
can suffer as a result of disobedience or ignorance. You
cannot escape problems and difficulties in life. You can,
however, choose to be an overcomer and to rise above the
problems and difficulties.

The Apostle Paul Suffered for the Right Reasons

The Apostle Paul lived a life where he had to endure
many hardships. He suffered from many relentless attacks
from a messenger of Satan. This evil force violently
harassed him on his journeys. He was shipwrecked. He
experienced fierce opposition to his ministry by angry
Jews. He was beaten and whipped and left for dead. He

suffered for doing good (2 Corinthians 11:23-29). However, The Apostle Paul was able to say with confidence the Lord delivered him from all his hardships.

> Persecutions, afflictions, which came unto me at Antioch, at Iconium, at Lystra; what persecutions I endured: but out of them all the Lord delivered me. (2 Timothy 3:11)

The Apostle Paul even boasted in his own weakness. He believed the Lord's strength would carry him through his weaknesses. He realized he was made more than a conqueror through Christ who loved him.

Many people misunderstand what it means to suffer for the Lord. The Apostle Paul suffered for the Lord. He was persecuted for his faith. To suffer for the Lord is a trial of your faith. Temptations and hardships come to test your faith, but with faith and patience you can overcome all your hardships.

Do Not Suffer Needlessly

Most people do not understand the difference between suffering for righteousness and suffering for foolishness. Suffering that is noble is suffering persecution because of doing good. Suffering that is needless is suffering that occurs when you disobey God and sin.

Suffering for your faith like the apostles and martyrs is an honorable type of suffering. Suffering because you misunderstand the goodness of God, or because you continue to sin, is suffering for the wrong reasons.

> If ye be reproached for the name of Christ, happy are ye; for the spirit of glory and of God resteth upon you: on their part he is evil spoken of, but on your part he is glorified. But let none of you

> suffer as a murderer, or as a thief, or as an evildoer, or as a busybody in other men's matters. Yet if any man suffer as a Christian, let him not be ashamed; but let him glorify God on this behalf.
>
> (1 Peter 4:14-16)

The devil comes and tempts you with evil. He is trying to stop your faith from working. He wants to entangle you in sin. Sin creates problems and limits in your life that are avoidable. Suffering for the wrong reason causes needless pain and hardship on you and others.

> For what glory is it, if, when ye be buffeted for your faults, ye shall take it patiently? but if, when ye do well, and suffer for it, ye take it patiently, this is acceptable with God. (1 Peter 2:20)

If you have made mistakes and sinned, God has made a way for you to purify yourself and receive forgiveness.

> If we confess our sins, he is faithful and just to forgive us our sins, and to cleanse us from all unrighteousness. (1 John 1:9-10)

Asking God to forgive you and then forsaking your sins settles the issue. This puts you back in right standing with God. You have become righteous and forgiven. You are blameless in His sight. He sees you through the righteousness of His Son Jesus. You have the right to come boldly into God's presence to find the help you need.

Most Christians today suffer for the wrong reasons. They suffer not because they are being persecuted for being good. They suffer because of doing things they should not do, or they suffer as a result of spiritual blindness. Spiritual blindness keeps people from knowing or believing the promises of God. Lack of knowledge about the rights, privileges, and blessings available to you through Jesus can open the door for the devil to destroy you.

> My people are destroyed for lack of knowledge: because thou hast rejected knowledge, I will also reject thee, that thou shalt be no priest to me: seeing thou hast forgotten the law of thy God, I will also forget thy children. (Hosea 4:6)

God does not promise you a life free from problems. He does not promise that you will not suffer. However, he does not desire you to suffer for the wrong reasons.

Suffering for the wrong reasons is a problem that imposes limits upon the believer. If we are going to experience the blessing of no more limits in our lives, we have to learn to discern God's will in suffering and hardships. You should avoid suffering needlessly.

CONQUERING TESTS AND HARDSHIPS THROUGH JESUS

* * *

Jesus Overcame the Devil

Jesus came to be a blessing to those around him. Jesus wanted people to enjoy the blessings of a loving Father. Jesus also came into the world to battle the darkness. Jesus was tempted by the devil. Jesus overcame the limits of the devil's tests and hardships and earned the right to be called more than a conqueror.

Jesus defeated the devil. We do not have to defeat the devil. He has already been defeated. However, the devil has not yet been removed from the earth. His work and his followers are still active in the world today. There are spiritual battles taking place around us all the time. We still have to fight the good fight of faith, but we will always be triumphant because of Jesus.

Submit Yourself to God, Resist the Devil and He will Flee

The Apostle Paul in Ephesians uses the illustration of

a battle ready soldier to describe the situations of life. He says to put on the armor of God to be able to withstand all the evil in the world (Ephesians 6:10-18). The Apostle Paul acknowledges the evil powers. He knew his enemy. He said:

> For we wrestle not against flesh and blood, but against principalities, against powers, against the rulers of the darkness of this world, against spiritual wickedness in high places.
>
> (Ephesians 6:12)

The Apostle Paul knew you would be involved in spiritual battles. You are to wear the armor of God to stand against the tactics of your spiritual enemy, the devil. God wants you to be victorious over all the spiritual attacks of the enemy. You can be strong in the power of God and be able to withstand the attacks

The Apostle James also describes how to win spiritual battles. He offers some practical advice when he says:

> Submit yourselves therefore to God. Resist the devil, and he will flee from you. (James 4:7)

The Apostle James' advice is simple. Submit yourself to God. Resist the devil and he will leave you alone. Resisting the devil is important. You must learn how to resist him and to fight against him. You must resist his attempts to steal, kill and destroy.

The words of the Apostle Paul and the Apostle James do not sound like the words of men who were used to being defeated by the devil. Their words sound like the words of experienced followers of Jesus telling us how we can overcome the attacks of the devil.

You Can Overcome the Limits of All Tests and Hardships

Tests and hardships come to limit your life. God can

help you overcome your tests and hardships. God has the solution for every test and hardship known to man. God has the answer to all your problems. Your answers are found in the victory and triumph of Jesus Christ over all the limits of the devil.

The Apostle Peter said you have an adversary roaming about seeking to devour you and you should resist him (1 Peter 5:8-9). The Apostle Peter also said:

> The Lord knoweth how to deliver the godly
> out of temptations, and to reserve the unjust unto
> the day of judgment to be punished: (2 Peter 2:9)

Temptations are tests and hardships. When you look to Jesus, He can help you through all your tests and hardships. Jesus experienced and overcame all the limits of the devil and the world. Through Jesus, you can overcome all your temptations.

You are not the only one who has ever had to experience tests and hardships. Everyone experiences these things. The Apostle Paul says:

> There hath no temptation taken you but such
> as is common to man: but God is faithful, who will
> not suffer you to be tempted above that ye are able;
> but will with the temptation also make a way to
> escape, that ye may be able to bear it.
>
> (1 Corinthians 10:13)

Jesus' victory allows you to walk in His victory parade and appropriate His resources to overcome the limits of all the tests and hardships you will ever experience.

Jesus Came to Destroy the Works of the Devil

Sickness, poverty and crime are all tests and hardships caused by the devil. Jesus came to destroy the works of the devil.

> He that committeth sin is of the devil; for the devil sinneth from the beginning. For this purpose the Son of God was manifested, that he might destroy the works of the devil.
>
> (1 John 3:8)

Jesus came to give you power to overcome all the power of the enemy. This includes all sickness, disease, poverty and death.

> And the seventy returned again with joy, saying, Lord, even the devils are subject unto us through thy name. And he said unto them, I beheld Satan as lightning fall from heaven. Behold, I give unto you power to tread on serpents and scorpions, and over all the power of the enemy: and nothing shall by any means hurt you.
>
> (Luke 10:17-19)

You Are More Than A Conqueror Over Tests and Hardships

The Apostle Paul emphatically stated that through all the tests and hardships of life you are more than a conqueror through a loving God who is always ready to help you. The Apostle Paul said you are not a helpless sheep being led to slaughter. He said you are more than a conqueror through Jesus who loved you.

> Who shall separate us from the love of Christ? shall tribulation, or distress, or persecution, or famine, or nakedness, or peril, or sword? As it is written, For thy sake we are killed all the day long; we are accounted as sheep for the slaughter.
>
> Nay, in all these things we are more than conquerors through him that loved us.
>
> (Romans 8:37-38)

CHAPTER 7

THE UNLIMITED POWER WITHIN

GOD'S POWER IS DORMANT WITHIN YOU

* * *

As a Christian you have been given spiritual power to live life victoriously. This type of power cannot be seen with the natural eyes, but others can see the effects of this power around you. The Holy Spirit lives on the inside of all Christians. The Holy Spirit is all-powerful, and He wants to express Himself through you.

Some people are carriers of dormant viruses. These viruses could be activated at any time and bring death and misery. Most people would believe a doctor if he tells them they have a deadly virus on the inside of them. However, when a preacher tells them the power of God is on the inside of them, they do not believe it. Most people will not believe the preacher, but they will believe the doctor. This should not be. You should believe the power of God is on the inside of you.

The power of God on the inside of you is much more powerful than you can imagine. It is the same power that is available to help you proclaim the Good News of Jesus to a dying world.

> But ye shall receive power, after that the Holy
> Ghost is come upon you: and ye shall be witnesses
> unto me both in Jerusalem, and in all Judaea, and
> in Samaria, and unto the uttermost part of the
> earth. (Acts 1:8).

The power of God on the inside of you strengthens your body and helps you overcome the effects of your human weaknesses:

> For though he was crucified through weak-
> ness, yet he liveth by the power of God. For we
> also are weak in him, but we shall live with him by
> the power of God toward you.
>
> (2 Corinthians 13:4).

The power of God on the inside of you enables you to receive from God whatever you need. This is the power that makes it possible for God to say he can do more than you could ever ask or imagine.

> Now unto him that is able to do exceeding
> abundantly above all that we ask or think, accord-
> ing to the power that worketh in us,
>
> (Ephesians 3:20).

The power of God on the inside of you is full of life. The power of God on the inside of you allows you to enter into the realm of no more limits. The more you understand about how God's power is made available to you through Jesus, the more you will be able to tap into it for your needs and the needs of others.

Knowledge Activates the Power of God

Your body has natural defenses. These defenses are known as your immune system. There are germs in the air and all around you. If you did not have a good immune system, you would die quickly. Germs may enter your body, but because your immune system protects you, you may never know it. If you have a strong immune system, it attacks germs that enter your body before they can harm you.

Similarly, the power of God is on the inside of you and helps you to fend off harmful attacks against you spiritually. All Christians have power on the inside of them that is available to help them when they need it. Studying the word of God helps you to know this power on the inside of you. Knowledge of God's will for your life activates this power.

> Grace and peace be multiplied unto you through the knowledge of God, and of Jesus our Lord, According as his divine power hath given unto us all things that pertain unto life and godliness, through the knowledge of him that hath called us to glory and virtue: (2 Peter 1:2-3).

Peter uses the past tense in this verse when he says that God *hath given unto us all things that pertain unto life and godliness*. "Hath given" is in the past tense. This means it is already done. This power is already available and ready to assist you in your life. Paul also uses the phrase "all things" which means, literally, that every single thing you need for life can be obtained by the power that works in you.

You should come to the place spiritually where you automatically react to things that oppose you. You should have a spiritual immune system that helps you in time of need. When the Word of God renews your mind, you can tell what things are from God and what things are not. If you do not have knowledge of God, you will not be able to fight against those things that are contrary to the will of God. If you have knowledge of God, your spiritual immune system will have the power to keep you from missing what God has for you.

Notice that the Scripture in 2 Peter 1:3 says the power of God has been given to those He has called to glory and virtue. Your calling is important. When you are fulfilling the calling on your life, you will see the results of the power of God. You will find yourself receiving all the things you need for life and Godliness.

To receive the fulfillment of this promise, you have to have knowledge of God. You have to apply the Word of God to your life. You have to study and gain knowledge. You also have to guard your heart to keep yourself from missing the will of God.

> My son, attend to my words; incline thine ear unto my sayings. Let them not depart from thine eyes; keep them in the midst of thine heart. For they are life unto those that find them, and health to all their flesh. Keep thy heart with all diligence; for out of it are the issues of life.
> (Proverbs 4:20-23).

There is a power working in you to fulfill God's purpose for your life. You need to apply the Word of God to your life. God has already given you all things that pertain to life and godliness. God is not holding anything back from you. God gave you everything when He sent Jesus to die for your sins. God demonstrated His love for you when He raised Jesus from the dead and gave you rights as a member of His family.

The Bible is like a will that designates you as the beneficiary. Imagine if you were to wake up one day and discover a long lost relative had left you a large sum of money in their will. The Bible is much more than a will from a rich relative. The Bible is a will from the ruler of the universe. God has promised you He has given you everything that pertains to life and Godliness

The Bible is God's will for your life. It tells you what legally belongs to you in the kingdom of God. The Bible is a road map for living. The Bible is a guide to help you know what belongs to you. The Bible also tells you how to receive what is rightfully yours. God takes His word and activates it with the power of the Holy Spirit that is on the inside of you. The Holy Spirit enables you to understand and know the will of God for your life.

The same Holy Spirit that created the universe is on the inside of you. You have an unlimited resource available to you in the person of the Holy Spirit. Spend time learning about the person of the Holy Spirit and how He wants to work and move in your life. The Holy Spirit is the power that will help you overcome all limits. The Holy Spirit will help you learn and understand the will of God for your life. The Holy Spirit will help you live a life that glorifies God.

You Are Called, Justified and Glorified

I mentioned this in Chapter 1 and it is worth repeating here. God has a predetermined plan for your life. He has called, justified and glorified you (Romans 8:30). He has called you to glory and virtue (2 Peter 1:3). What does it mean to be called to glory and virtue?

Paul is saying God has put His glory in you when you became a Christian. The Holy Spirit lives on the inside of you. The Holy Spirit is a gift from God to help you lead a life of virtue that gives glory to God (John 16:5-15). When we do things that bring glory to God, we are fulfilling His plan for our lives. Doing good works and living triumphantly through Christ brings glory to God. Living a life that expresses the power of God brings glory to God.

When you became a Christian, God fixed you spiritually to hold His power. You were broken and helpless spiritually before Christ. After Christ removed your sins, He gave you a new spiritual life. He put His glory and His power on the inside of you. He has told you He has given you all you need to be successful in this life. He wants you to experience His abundant life. You need to activate the power of the Holy Spirit on the inside of you. You activate the power of the Holy Spirit by gaining knowledge about God and then acting in faith upon what you know.

You Receive God's Nature Through His Promises

God has given you promises so that you might receive a new life and a new nature. These promises allow you to escape the evil in the world.

> **Whereby are given unto us exceeding great and precious promises: that by these ye might be partakers of the divine nature, having escaped the corruption that is in the world through lust.**
>
> **(2 Peter 1:4).**

Here is the word "exceeding" again. God has given you unlimited promises. He has given these promises to you so you can have his nature and power in your life.

You can partake of God's divine nature. This is a tremendous promise. Some people misunderstand this. It does not say you will be God, it says you will be like God. In other words, you can act like Him in certain situations.

I'm not God but I will be like God by his promise

If you are a Christian, you are born of God. If you are born of God, you have certain precious promises that allow you to act like your Brother Jesus in certain situations. God has given you promises, and you can use them to glorify Him.

God says you can be a partaker of His divine nature, but the way you are going to partake of His nature is through His promises. God's precious promises are found in the Bible, the Word of God.

You Partake of God's Promises by Being Fully Persuaded

Abraham was given precious promises. God promised Abraham he would be blessed and become a blessing to the whole world. Abraham was promised a child by his wife Sarah. This would be a miracle because Abraham was 100 years old and Sarah was 90 years old, well past her time of being able to conceive a child (Genesis 17:17). Abraham did not stagger at the promises of God. Abraham had great faith. The Apostle Paul mentions Abraham's faith in this passage in Romans.

> **And being fully persuaded that, what he had promised, he was able also to perform.**
>
> **(Romans 4:21)**

The Apostle Paul is describing how Abraham was persuaded God was going to bless him with a child through Sarah. God had given him a promise and he believed God at His word. Sarah had a child, and Abraham became the father of many nations (Genesis 21:2). One of Abraham's descendants was Jesus Christ.

When you believe God's promises are true, even when the circumstances look bad, you are demonstrating faith in God. Abraham was fully persuaded God's promises were true. You can be fully persuaded God's promises are true, and you can be blessed.

Here is the key to partaking of God's divine nature. God has given you promises. God also has given you the power to believe His promises. God's promises are activated when you are fully persuaded God is able to do what He said He could do. This is the key to entering into a life where God is able to do exceeding abundantly above all you can ask or imagine. When you have faith in God's promises, the power of the Holy Spirit works in you and through you to bring them to pass.

When you read and act on the promises of God that are His will for your life, you can be fully persuaded He can fulfill His promises. The more you meditate on the promises found in the Bible, the more you will be persuaded God is able and willing to bring them to pass.

We have read in 2 Peter 1:4 where the promises will help you escape the corruption and lust in the world. If you are fully persuaded, you will not act on the temptation to be drawn away in unbelief. If you are fully persuaded, you will not act on thoughts of worry, fear or failure. The Holy Spirit, the power of God working in you, keeps you from falling into the traps of the enemy.

Overcoming Limits on the Power of God

There are times when the power of God is limited in your life. This entire book is written for the purpose of helping you remove the limits that are keeping you from experiencing the life God has for you.

We talked about limits in Chapter 3. Limits are boundaries that keep us separated from the resources of heaven. There are three more limits that I will discuss that limit the power of God in our lives. These limits have to do with our attitudes. The three limits are the attitude of

3 Things limit.
attitude

unworthiness, the attitude of false humility, and the attitude of being offended.

We need to change our attitudes and renew our minds with the Word of God. This frees us to receive what God has planned for us. This frees us and allows us to operate in the unlimited power of the Holy Spirit that is within us.

Unworthiness

An attitude of unworthiness can be a product of guilt, condemnation or failure. Unworthiness can also be a product of wrong doctrine. People can teach you that you are unworthy. They can say you are like an old unworthy worm in the dust. You are just an unworthy pilgrim trudging through life in the heat and the cold. You are not worth anything. God saved you, but you still are a sorry, no-good mess.

If you hear this unworthy message long enough, you will leave church lower than you came. After years and years of that, you will think you are not worth anything to God or anyone else. This type of wrong teaching and wrong thinking causes you to put limits on yourself.

These limits keep you from believing you are worthy to receive anything from God. You will not think you have any value, and you will think God does not care about you. You will not think God wants to do anything for you. You might think He loves your pastor or some famous preacher, but you are not sure He loves you.

All people have the same background. We were all sinners. We were all unworthy to receive the blessings of God. Not one of us was righteous by ourselves before God. Fortunately for all of us, Jesus died for our sins. God loved us so much that He sent Jesus to pay the price for our sins. When we accepted Jesus Christ as Lord of our lives, He put a new life on the inside of us. This new life has value because it is born of God.

When God gave you a new life, He took away the old and gave you something new. Your new life is based upon what Jesus has done for you. You were unworthy to approach God on your own behalf, but Jesus prepared a way for you to be brought into the presence of God.

Jesus is the door for you to enter into the blessings of God. You became like Jesus when you accepted Him as your Lord. You are now worthy to be used for the glory of God. To say you are not worthy to be used of God is to ignore who you are in Christ. You are no longer a sinner saved by grace. You were a sinner, you were saved by grace, and you have become the righteousness of God in Christ.

> For he hath made him to be sin for us, who knew no sin; that we might be made the righteousness of God in him.   (2 Corinthians 5:21).

You can do nothing in yourself, but through Jesus Christ you are made the righteousness of God. You have become something valuable and precious. God has sent the Holy Spirit to live in you and to give you power to do God's will. You were bought with a price and you should not live selfishly, but you should glorify God in all your actions.

> What? know ye not that your body is the temple of the Holy Ghost which is in you, which ye have of God, and ye are not your own? For ye are bought with a price: therefore glorify God in your body, and in your spirit, which are God's.
> (1 Corinthians 6:19-20).

You are valuable and precious to God. You are worth something because God paid for your redemption from your sins with the blood of His only Son Jesus. You were bought with a price, and now you should feel obligated to glorify God. You are made worthy to be blessed by God, and you have been made worthy to be a blessing to others. Your value outside of Jesus is nothing. Your value with Jesus is priceless.

There will always be people who are limited by their religious traditions. These people are the unworthy bunch. They are the "mud pots for Jesus." They feel that their unworthiness is a badge of honor. They fail to see the reality of what Jesus has made them. They are not unworthy if they are born again. If the Holy Spirit has given them life, they have been made worthy by the death of Jesus.

When you start saying you are worthy to be blessed, the unworthy religious bunch may disagree with you and accuse you of being arrogant. It is not arrogant to accept the gift of grace God has given you. You are not worthy because you have done anything yourself. You are worthy because of what Jesus did. He made you worthy by His death. All the glory goes to God.

When you understand you are worthy because of Jesus, you are on your way to removing the limit of "unworthiness." Removing this limit will help you to receive all God has planned for you.

False Humility

An attitude of false humility is different from an attitude of unworthiness. Unworthiness is a result of bad doctrines, problems or upbringing, but false humility is a form of pride. Pride is a limit that keeps you from being blessed by God.

93

False humility is trying to be something you are not. You do not believe you are humble, but you are acting humble to impress others. False humility is phony. If you have an attitude of false humility, you need to eliminate it so you can be who God wants you to be and do what God wants you to do.

> **Likewise, ye younger, submit yourselves unto the elder. Yea, all of you be subject one to another, and be clothed with humility: for God resisteth the proud, and giveth grace to the humble.**
>
> **(1 Peter 5:5).**

Real humility is an honorable attribute. False humility is a stench in the nostrils of God. God will not bless pride and arrogance. Let go of false humility and walk in true humility, and God will exalt you in due season.

> **Humble yourselves therefore under the mighty hand of God, that he may exalt you in due time:** **(1 Peter 5:6).**

True humility is acting on who you are in Christ. You realize you can do nothing in your own strength. It is through the power of God on the inside of you that you will become and do what God has planned. True humility is a beautiful thing and demonstrates that you know your place before God. Your place before God is based upon who you are in Christ and not upon who you are in yourself.

Being Easily Offended

Many people limit God because they become offended. Being offended is developing a wrong attitude toward God or Jesus or someone else. Offenses are a trap placed by the enemy to limit the power of God from operating in your life.

I believe most people today could not handle Jesus if they were to hear Him speak. If He pastored a church, He would probably run many folks away. He would only speak the truth in love, but most people would be offended by His truthfulness.

I often say things in love to people to try to help them and it sometimes upsets them. I try to say things as lovingly as I know how, but there are just some people who have an "offense meter" that is very sensitive. People will run away from the truth because they love the darkness more than the light.

Walking in love means you will forgive people. Forgiveness is a powerful force that takes the limits off God.

> And when ye stand praying, forgive, if ye have ought against any: that your Father also which is in heaven may forgive you your trespasses. But if ye do not forgive, neither will your Father which is in heaven forgive your trespasses.
>
> (Mark 11:25-26).

Letting go of offenses and walking in the truth and love of God will allow you to experience more of the unlimited power of God within you.

What You Do Affects How People View God

Whether you want to believe it or not, when people are looking at you as a Christian, they form an opinion about God. God has called you to be His representative. You are an ambassador for Christ.

> Now then we are ambassadors for Christ, as though God did beseech you by us: we pray you in Christ's stead, be ye reconciled to God.
>
> (2 Corinthians 5:20).

I understand this is a sensitive area in some people's

lives. I must say it. How you live your life as a Christian gives other people an impression about God.

If you limit God in your life, you will cause others to have a limited perspective of God. If you are limiting God by attitudes of unworthiness or false humility, you will give people the wrong idea about God. If you are easily offended and have unforgiveness in your life, you will portray this to others. When you limit God in your own life through wrong attitudes and behaviors, you limit God in the eyes of others.

When people see you, what do they learn about God? Do you represent God well?

Some people look at the way many Christians live and want to have nothing to do with God. When they see you poor, they think that God is poor. When they see you prospering, they think that God is prospering. Right or wrong, that influences people. When you are blessed in all areas of your life, when you are walking in health, and when you are prospering financially, you are an example to others.

Please be careful with this. You should not want to be blessed to keep up with what other people are doing. You can become greedy and love money and hurt yourself. You should want to be blessed by God for the right reasons. You should want to be blessed to glorify God and to be able to help others. God wants you to be blessed, but your priorities need to be right.

> **But seek ye first the kingdom of God, and his righteousness; and all these things shall be added unto you.** (Matthew 6:33).

When your priorities are in the proper perspective,

you can be blessed in all areas of your life. When you are obedient to God and serving Him with good intentions, then you will be able to be an example for others to follow. This does not mean you will never have problems. This does not mean you will never suffer persecution or afflictions. This means that you will have the power working on the inside of you that allows you to bring glory to God through all your circumstances.

> **Fear not, little flock; for it is your Father's good pleasure to give you the kingdom.**
>
> **(Luke 12:32).**

It gives God pleasure to bless you. If you could just understand how God is more than willing to do exceeding abundantly above all you could ask or think, your limits would be shattered.

> **Now unto him that is able to do exceeding abundantly above all that we ask or think, according to the power that worketh in us, Unto him be glory in the church by Christ Jesus throughout all ages, world without end. Amen.**
>
> **(Ephesians 3:20-21).**

God makes this all possible by the power He has given you through the Holy Sprit who lives in you. You are the temple of the Holy Spirit. You are the container of God's power. When you lay hands on the sick, He is laying hands on the sick. When you feed the hungry, and clothe the naked, He is doing it through you. He wants you to remove your limits so He can use you to bring glory to Himself through your life and actions. This is all made possible by the unlimited power of the Holy Spirit within you.

THE UNLIMITED POTENTIAL OF PRAYER

GOD IS WILLING TO HELP YOU

* * *

Christians are often limited in their prayer lives because they do not understand how willing God is to meet their needs. Everyone is confident of God's ability to do anything, but not everyone is sure He is willing to do it for them today. We need to connect God's willingness and ability together. God is willing to do anything we ask that will bring glory to Him.

> And whatsoever ye shall ask in my name, that will I do, that the Father may be glorified in the Son.   (John 14:13).

God wants to answer your prayer so He may be glorified through Jesus. God is able and willing to answer your prayers.

One of the most precious stories to me in the Bible is the man who came to Jesus to seek cleansing from his disease of leprosy. I have ministered in two leper colonies, and I have heard the cry in those people's hearts and have seen the agony in their bodies. Lepers often have fingers, ears and noses that have been eaten away by the disease. The leper's appearance makes them repulsive to most people and they are social outcasts. It would be repulsive for most people to consider touching a person with leprosy.

Leprosy has been around for thousands of years. In ancient Israel lepers were considered unclean and were forced to live away from most people. Whenever a leper went out in public he had to cry out in a loud voice, "Unclean! Unclean!" Lepers were not allowed to associate with anyone except other lepers. Only out of desperation did this leper approach Jesus. We can still hear this leper's desperate plea for help from the book of Mark.

> **And there came a leper to him, beseeching him, and kneeling down to him, and saying unto him, If thou wilt, thou canst make me clean.**
>
> **(Mark 1:40).**

This leper had heard of the marvelous things Jesus had done for others. He heard of His miraculous abilities and how He had healed many others. He knew Jesus was able to heal him. However, he was not sure if Jesus was willing to heal a man like him.

This leper represents all of us. We were all unclean and unworthy to approach God on our own merits. Paul says in Romans 3:23, *All have sinned and fallen short of the glory of God.* We all need a Savior to cleanse us from our sins and to make us clean. We know Jesus can cleanse our hearts, but is He willing to help us with other needs in our lives?

Let us look at how Jesus responded to this man's plea for help.

> And Jesus, moved with compassion, put forth
> his hand, and touched him, and saith unto him, I
> will; be thou clean.   (Mark 1:41).

Jesus reached out and touched this man and said, "I will, be thou clean." Jesus demonstrated he was not only able but also willing to heal him. He reached out in love and touched this man whom no one else was willing to touch. Jesus touched him and answered his prayer. Jesus cleansed him from his leprosy.

Jesus is willing to help you. Whatever you are asking for, if it will glorify Jesus, God is able and willing to give it to you. God is willing to help you with whatever you ask. It does not have to be physical healing. It can be emotional healing. It can be love. It can be anything you need.

You Can Ask God for Anything According to His Will

God wants you to have your prayers met. He wants you to know He will grant you whatever you ask. However, there is one important condition. God will only answer your prayer when you ask for something that is His will.

> And this is the confidence that we have in
> him, that, if we ask any thing according to his will,
> he heareth us: And if we know that he hear us,
> whatsoever we ask, we know that we have the peti-
> tions that we desired of him.   (1 John 5:14-15).

Notice the words "whatsoever we ask." Whatsoever means anything. There are no limits to what you can ask when you are asking according to what God has willed for you.

What is the Will of the Lord?

I have heard some people pray and add the expression

101

"if it be thy will Lord" to the end of all their prayers. People are not really sure what the will of God is and they use this as a blanket statement to cover themselves if their prayers are not answered. When you add this to the end of a prayer, you are saying you are not sure what the will of God is in this situation.

Jesus prayed for God's will to be done and not His own. The cup he speaks of in the following verse is symbolic of his suffering and death.

> Saying, Father, if thou be willing, remove this
> cup from me: nevertheless not my will, but thine,
> be done.   (Luke 22:42).

The will of God was for Jesus to die on the cross. There was no other way to redeem humanity from sin, sickness, poverty and death except by dying on the cross. God's will was for Jesus to suffer and die for your sins. His death and suffering made it possible for you to be made an overcomer and to receive abundant life. You always know it is God's will to save people.

> For whosoever shall call upon the name of the
> Lord shall be saved.   (Romans 10:13).

A sinner never has to pray, "If it be thy will Lord, save me." It is God's will to save sinners. Any person, who is willing to change their life, and who asks God to save them, will be saved. A simple prayer of faith saying, "God save me!" is all that is necessary.

The initial prayer of salvation opens the door to more than a ticket to heaven. Salvation allows Jesus to come and live with us in our hearts. Salvation brings a change in lifestyle. Salvation entitles the believer to wholeness, restoration and eternal life.

Traditions of men limit God by through prayers of

"Lord heal me, if it be thy will" or "Lord meet my daily financial needs, if it be thy will." If it is clearly God's will in the Bible, it is clearly God's will for your life. Do not let tradition rob you from knowing God's will for your life. Read your Bible prayerfully, and you will know His will for you concerning healing and having your needs met.

Is God's Will Always Done?

God's will is not always done. It is not God's will for any person to die and go to hell.

> **The Lord is not slack concerning his promise, as some men count slackness; but is longsuffering to us-ward, not willing that any should perish, but that all should come to repentance. (2 Peter 3:9).**

Do people go to hell? Yes, people go to hell against God's will every day. Jesus said the road to hell is a broad road and the road to life is narrow (Matthew 7:13-14). Multitudes of people are on the broad road to hell against God's will for their lives.

People use their own free will to reject the will of God. You can choose not to accept the will of God for your life, and God will honor your wishes. Because it is God's will for a person to be saved or blessed in an area does not mean that His will is being done. You have to recognize and receive God's will by faith.

When people die and go to hell against the will of God, this does not change the will of God. God will save whoever calls on the name of the Lord (Romans 10:13). Someone who dies of cancer does not change the will of God concerning healing. The fact that by His stripes you were healed is still true (1 Peter 2:24). Someone who goes bankrupt does not change the will of God. The fact that God shall supply all your needs according to His riches in glory through Christ Jesus is still true (Philippians 4:19). Someone who commits adultery or steals does not change the will of God. God does not endorse sin. People sin against the will of God all the time. The sinful actions or inaction of others does not change the will of God for your life.

You have been given a free will to choose what you believe and what you do not believe. You should choose to serve and obey God. Joshua chose to serve and follow God. Joshua said in a speech to the Israelites:

> And if it seem evil unto you to serve the LORD, choose you this day whom ye will serve; whether the gods which your fathers served that were on the other side of the flood, or the gods of the Amorites, in whose land ye dwell: but as for me and my house, we will serve the LORD.
> (Joshua 24:12-15).

You and those in your house should choose to receive and obey the will of God. Obedience to God will result in the fulfillment of all God's promises concerning your life. When you obey God and are serving Him according to His will, all things will work together for your good (Romans 8:28).

Many Traditions Nullify the Will of the Lord

There are religious traditions that declare many things are no longer God's will. You know you are in trouble when religious men go to great lengths to explain why the Bible does not mean what it says. Religious tradition nullifies what the Bible says.

Traditions admit the Bible is true, but then nullify the word of God by saying it is not true for you today. Traditions say, "It is no longer God's will to heal today" and "Miracles have ceased."

Other traditions admit God wants to bless you spiritually, but they stop short of saying God can help you pay your rent or fix your car. They say you can never be sure if God is willing to help you with anything that is not spiritual. They say, "You can never be sure of the will of the Lord."

Traditions set limits on what people expect God to do for them. People have asked God for things and did not receive them. Out of their experiences they develop doctrine. Because they did not receive exactly what they prayed for, they assumed it must not have been God's will. They say, "I asked God for a new washing machine, and I got a scrub board. It must be God didn't want me to have that expensive washing machine." They put their experience above the Word of God and came to the wrong conclusion.

Another example might be in the area of healing. A person may say, "I prayed for my aunt to be healed from cancer and she died." The conclusion from this experience may be, "It must not be God's will to heal today." Many people look to the circumstances to determine the will of God. The Word of God is a higher authority than circumstances. The word of God is true in spite of many traditions that say healing is no longer for today.

People may base their faith upon what has happened to others, or people may base their faith upon the promises of God. The Bible is full of promises. You will not be disappointed basing your faith upon the Bible. You will be disappointed basing your faith upon what happened to so-and-so.

Jesus came and triumphed over sin, sickness, poverty, and over all the power of the devil. It is not the will of God for a child of God to be subjected to a life under the power of the devil. God's will for your life is to be a victorious overcomer over all the power of the enemy. God's will for your life is to reign in life over your circumstances. You reign in life by his grace and righteousness through Jesus Christ (Romans 5:17).

Thy Will Be Done in Earth as It Is in Heaven

The will of God is clear when you use the Bible as your guide. What is God's will for you? Jesus taught his disciples to pray that God's will be done on earth as it is in heaven.

> After this manner therefore pray ye: Our Father which art in heaven, Hallowed be thy name. Thy kingdom come. Thy will be done in earth, as it is in heaven. Give us this day our daily bread.
> (Matthew 6:9-11).

This passage is part of what we call the Lord's Prayer. It really should be called the disciple's prayer. Jesus taught his disciples this prayer to help guide them in their prayer life.

Think for a minute about the statement, "Thy will be done in earth as it is in heaven." Jesus said we could pray for God's will to be done on earth as it is in heaven. If you look at the Bible and see how wonderful things are in heaven, this gives you some idea of what God's will might be for you.

Is there sickness and disease in heaven? Of course not. Everything is healthy in heaven. Is there poverty in heaven? Of course not. The streets are paved in gold. Are there heartbreaks and disappointments in heaven? No, there is happiness and joy. If God's will be done on earth as it was in heaven, there would be no sickness, no disease, no poverty, and no sorrow. There would be health, prosperity and joy.

God is Able to Do More For You than You Can Ask or Think

God stands ready willing and able to answer your prayers. The Apostle Paul summed it all up when he said:

> Now unto him that is able to do exceeding abundantly above all that we ask or think, according to the power that worketh in us, Unto him be glory in the church by Christ Jesus throughout all ages, world without end. Amen.
>
> (Ephesians 3:20-21).

God is able to do exceeding abundantly more than you can ask or think according to the power that works in you. Many people today are still asking, "Is it God's will to heal me." Is it God's will to bless me financially? Is it God's will for me to have the finances to be able to help others? God has given us His will. God's will is written in the words of the Bible. If the Bible says you can have something, this is the will of God of God for you.

Your Heavenly Father Wants You to Ask for Good Things

God wants you to ask for good things. He wants you to have the things that you need in your life. You must seek and knock on the door of heaven. God has promised that when you seek, you will find. He will open the door of heaven and give you what you need.

> Ask, and it shall be given you; seek, and ye shall find; knock, and it shall be opened unto you: For every one that asketh receiveth; and he that seeketh findeth; and to him that knocketh it shall be opened. Or what man is there of you, whom if his son ask bread, will he give him a stone? Or if he ask a fish, will he give him a serpent?
>
> (Matthew 7:7-10).

God is a good God and wants to give good things to His children. This does not sound as if God wants you to be limited. He wants you to have whatever you need.

Jesus used the illustration of bread. Bread is important to daily life. Bread represents the essentials of life, what is important to us. Bread could be money, love, healing, joy or whatever you need.

Now that does not sound to me as if God wants you limited. Jesus said ask and it will be given you. Seek and you will find. Knock and it will be opened to you. For everyone that asks receives and he that seeks finds. Knock and the door will be opened!

The Bible says that just as a human father wants to provide for his children, the Heavenly Father also wants to provide many good things for His children.

> **If ye then, being evil, know how to give good gifts unto your children, how much more shall your Father which is in heaven give good things to them that ask him?** (Matthew 7:11).

If children ask their father for bread, he will not give them stones. If they ask him for fish, he will not give them serpents. If earthly fathers want to give good things to their children, how much more does our heavenly Father want to give good things to His children who ask Him. God is not trying to see how little He can do for you; God is trying to see how much He can do for you.

We are Here to Do the Work of the Lord

I have read many books, and I have listened to many tapes about prosperity. I have studied this information, and I have come to the conclusion that prosperity's purpose is to finish the work that God has called us to do, and bless us in the process.

Prosperity's motive is not about amassing personal wealth and fortune for yourself. You cannot take your wealth with you. Wealth is temporary it is not eternal. It is only what you do with your wealth that is eternal.

We recently spent several thousand dollars feeding over 500 people a holiday dinner. Our money went for a good cause, and we were glad to be able to spend it. The food met a temporary need, but it was our motivation that was important. God was pleased with the motivation of our hearts and the results brought glory to Jesus.

Money in itself has no intrinsic value. It is what you do with the money that is going to count in eternity. Having resources and money is important to finish the work God has called you to do. You can be confident it is God's will to give you the money you need to do what He has predestined and called you to do.

These Principles Work in All Areas of Your Life

Now if asking God for money bothers you, then apply this principle and work on it in other areas of your life. Ask God for anything you need. Are you walking in all the love you want? Are you walking in all the peace that you desire? Do you have all the joy you can hold? Do you need more of these things in your life? Of course you do. These are things everyone needs.

Do Not Covet My Tie

I had a man walk up to me and say, "That tie looks sharp. I just claim that tie." That is not faith. That is coveting. That was my tie. God will not answer that prayer because that man was coveting someone else's possessions.

If I had that tie out on a rack for sale, or if I was giving it away, he could claim it. He cannot claim it as long as I am wearing it around my neck. You have to be honest and you have to realize, you cannot go around coveting something that belongs to someone else. You cannot expect God to bless you when you are going against His will. He says do not covet (Romans 13:9). If He said not to covet, He will not answer a prayer that is against His word. His Word is His will.

God Does Not Answer Selfish Prayers

God will not answer prayers that fulfill your lusts. You cannot ask God to give you things you will use to fulfill evil desires You must ask God for good things. Fulfilling the lust of your flesh is not a good thing,

God's will is not for you to fulfill the lusts of your flesh. His word tells us to be led by the Holy Spirit. When the Holy Spirit leads you, you will not be asking for things that go against God's will for your life.

> Ye lust, and have not: ye kill, and desire to have, and cannot obtain: ye fight and war, yet ye have not, because ye ask not. Ye ask, and receive not, because ye ask amiss, that ye may consume it upon your lusts.   (James 4:2-3).

James points out a problem. People ask for the wrong reasons. When you ask for selfish reasons, God does not answer those prayers. James also points out another problem. He says, "You have not, because you ask not." On one hand, you go to God and pray selfishly. On the other hand, you do not go to God unselfishly and ask for things you need. If you find out what God promises, and if you ask for the right reasons, God will give you whatever you ask.

There Are No Limits to the Promises of God

There are thousands of promises in the Bible. God has promises for every area of life. Relationships, jobs, money, health—you name it and God has a promise for it. Every need man has ever had, or will ever have, is covered by the promises of God in the Bible.

The Apostle Peter says in the following verses that you have been given everything you need that pertains to your life. He says the promises are great and precious.

> Grace and peace be multiplied unto you through the knowledge of God, and of Jesus our Lord, According as his divine power hath given unto us all things that pertain unto life and godliness, through the knowledge of him that hath called us to glory and virtue: Whereby are given unto us exceeding great and precious promises: that by these ye might be partakers of the divine nature, having escaped the corruption that is in the world through lust. (2 Peter 1:2-4).

The Bible uses the past tense when it says God "hath given unto us all things that pertain unto life and godliness." God has already given you what you need.

The more knowledge you have of Him, the more you realize what already belongs to you. God has called you to glory and virtue. When you have what you need, you escape the corruption caused by lust. Having what you need helps you to remain pure and full of truth.

Peter uses the word "exceeding" to describe the promises of God. Exceeding means excessive. Exceeding means without limits. God wants to bless you exceedingly so that you might experience His divine nature. He wants you to escape the lustful corruption that is around you.

He wants you to be like Jesus. He wants you to be blessed so you can be a blessing to others.

No More Limits in Prayer

God's Word is His will. The following verses mean what they say. These Scriptural promises are not just for the apostles. They are for you today!

> Verily, verily, I say unto you, He that believeth on me, the works that I do shall he do also; and greater works than these shall he do; because I go unto my Father. And whatsoever ye shall ask in my name, that will I do, that the Father may be glorified in the Son. If ye shall ask any thing in my name, I will do it. (John 14:12-14).

> And in that day ye shall ask me nothing. Verily, verily, I say unto you, Whatsoever ye shall ask the Father in my name, he will give it you. Hitherto have ye asked nothing in my name: ask, and ye shall receive, that your joy may be full.
> (John 16:23-24).

> And Jesus answering saith unto them, Have faith in God. For verily I say unto you, That whosoever shall say unto this mountain, Be thou removed, and be thou cast into the sea; and shall not doubt in his heart, but shall believe that those things which he saith shall come to pass; he shall have whatsoever he saith. Therefore I say unto you, What things soever ye desire, when ye pray, believe that ye receive them, and ye shall have them. (Mark 11:22-24).

> If ye abide in me, and my words abide in you, ye shall ask what ye will, and it shall be done unto you. Herein is my Father glorified, that ye bear much fruit; so shall ye be my disciples.
> (John 15:7-8).

Find Out What God Promises in His Word

You can ask for whatever God has promised in His Word. You must not limit God and what He can do in you and through you. You have been given exceeding great and precious promises.

Now what did God say you could have? What are some of these great and precious promises?

God promises salvation.

> For whosoever shall call upon the name of the Lord shall be saved (Romans 10:13).

God promises deliverance from trouble.

> And call upon me in the day of trouble: I will deliver thee, and thou shalt glorify me.
>
> (Psalms 50:15).

God promises forgiveness.

> If we confess our sins, he is faithful and just to forgive us our sins, and to cleanse us from all unrighteousness. (1 John 1:9).

God promises healing and forgiveness to anyone who is sick in the church.

> Is any sick among you? let him call for the elders of the church; and let them pray over him, anointing him with oil in the name of the Lord: And the prayer of faith shall save the sick, and the Lord shall raise him up; and if he have committed sins, they shall be forgiven him (James 5:14-15).

God promises freedom from fear, power, love and a sound mind.

> For God hath not given us the spirit of fear; but of power, and of love, and of a sound mind.
>
> (2 Timothy 1:7).

God promises wisdom to those who ask.

> If any of you lack wisdom, let him ask of God,
> that giveth to all men liberally, and upbraideth not;
> and it shall be given him   (James 1:5).

God promises that you can overcome covetousness, discontentment and loneliness.

> Let your conversation be without covetousness; and be content with such things as ye have: for he hath said, I will never leave thee, nor forsake thee.   (Hebrews 13:5).

God promises prosperity.

> Give, and it shall be given unto you; good measure, pressed down, and shaken together, and running over, shall men give into your bosom. For with the same measure that ye mete withal it shall be measured to you again.   (Luke 6:38).

God promises peace of mind and joy and hope.

> Now the God of hope fill you with all joy and peace in believing, that ye may abound in hope, through the power of the Holy Ghost.
>
> (Romans 15:13).

Anything God promises He will give you. That is His will for you. Any of these promises you can have. They are yours. He has given them to you and you can stand in faith for them.

If you ask anything according to His will, you know He hears you (1 John 5:14-15). Jesus said to ask the Father anything in His name and He will give it to you (John 16:23). As far as I am concerned, it is hard to beat a deal like that!

THE UNLIMITED RICHES OF GOD'S RESOURCES

THERE ARE NO MORE LIMITS TO GOD'S ABUNDANCE

* * *

You serve a God that is able to help you. You cannot ask or think above what God can do for you.

> Now unto him that is able to do exceeding abundantly above all that we ask or think, according to the power that worketh in us. (Ephesians 3:20)

We limit ourselves when we say God will not bless us like He blesses someone else. God is not like this. He will bless anyone who believes His promises. God is no respecter of persons (Romans 2:11). He does not have favorites. He is able to do exceeding abundantly for anyone who will not limit Him.

We limit God because we do not think He can or will do anything for us. We do not expect God to do anything for us, and we do not receive anything from Him. We fail to ask, because we fail to look beyond our limits. We fail to recognize the limitless abundance of God.

We limit God without realizing we are limiting him.

We allow God to bless us in some areas of our lives but not others. One of the hardest areas for most people to receive the abundance of God is in the area of finances.

When I start talking about God's abundance in finances, I lose some people. As soon as I start talking about money, some people tune me out. They think, "All that preacher ever wants to talk about is money. Those guys are just in this for the money."

This could not be further from the truth. I talk about money because money is important to God. Jesus said to put your treasure in a heavenly account. He said to store your treasure in heaven by giving to do the work of the ministry.

> **But lay up for yourselves treasures in heaven, where neither moth nor rust doth corrupt, and where thieves do not break through nor steal: For where your treasure is, there will your heart be also.** (Matthew 6:20-21).

Jesus spent much time talking about money. Money is important to people, and Jesus talked about it and used parables about money to illustrate principles in the Kingdom of God (Matthew 18:23-35; Luke 15:8-10, 16:1-13, 19:1-27). Jesus did not want you to trust in uncertain riches. You are to put your trust in Him (1 Timothy 6:17). God is more than able to meet your needs according to His riches in glory by Christ Jesus (Philippians 4:19).

The power of God brings you money (Deuteronomy 8:18). God is the source of your money supply, but money comes to you through someone's hands. God brings money to you through others when you are generous with what you possess (Luke 6:38).

It is sad to see money stand between somebody and God. All too often people will love the things of the world, and the things money will buy, instead of loving God and loving people. When someone loves their money more than they love God or other people, they have messed up priorities.

Money is not bad. The *love* of money is bad (1 Timothy 6:10). Money is necessary to live in this world. Jesus himself paid taxes (Matthew 17:24-27). Jesus had a treasurer to carry around a moneybag (John 13:29). Jesus was not without financial resources. Jesus had several wealthy women who followed Him and supported His ministry (Luke 8:1-3).

The Bible never says Jesus lived with a lack of finances. He had money for Judas to embezzle (John 12:6). Jesus had enough money that the disciples thought Judas was going out to help the poor when he was on his way to betray Jesus (John 13:27-29). Jesus was not poor until He made Himself poor on the cross. Jesus' poverty on the cross enables us to acquire spiritual and earthly riches to fulfill the purposes of God in our lives (2 Corinthians 8:9).

The Apostle Paul collected a large offering from the churches and took it to the church in Jerusalem to help them through some financial difficulties. He commended those who were eager to give to this offering (2 Corinthians 9:1-15).

The money is not what is important. It is what you do with the money that is important. The reason you should allow God to bless you financially is that it takes money to spread the ministry of Jesus Christ around the world. When you are blessed financially, you can be generous in helping others.

We need to change our way of thinking about money. We need to understand that the unlimited riches of God's glory applies to our finances as well as to everything else we need. Money allows us to accomplish what God has called us to do. Money is important to help us fulfill the will of God for our lives and our mission to serve others.

The Unlimited Resources of God

God allowed David to gather the resources to build a temple for the Lord in Jerusalem. God had David make the preparations for the temple his son Solomon would build. This temple was a magnificent work. It was built with an abundance of silver, gold, brass and the finest of cedar wood.

> And David prepared iron in abundance for the nails for the doors of the gates, and for the joinings; and brass in abundance without weight; Also cedar trees in abundance: for the Zidonians and they of Tyre brought much cedar wood to David.
>
> (1 Chronicles 22:3-4).

God provided an abundance of the supplies necessary to build the temple. This temple was where He would come down and dwell in the presence of His people. His glory would be in the innermost parts of this temple. God adorned this temple with valuable gold and silver. David describes the extensive wealth he made available for the temple. He said:

> Now, behold, in my trouble I have prepared for the house of the LORD an hundred thousand talents of gold, and a thousand thousand talents of silver; and of brass and iron without weight; for it is in abundance: timber also and stone have I prepared; and thou mayest add thereto.
>
> (1 Chronicles 22:14).

One hundred thousand talents of gold! References say this is about 3,800 tons. At the current price of gold this would be worth about $38 billion. The silver was a thousand, thousand talents of silver. That is one million talents or about 38,000 tons of silver. At today's prices that is worth about $7 billion. The total David gave was over $45 billion. This did not include the cost of the brass and iron which was too much to count. David's gift to the Lord far surpassed the generosity of the wealthiest billionaires of our time.

Doing the Lord's Work Takes Resources

When we talk about no more limits, we must always remember the whole thing is about mission not about money. If you do not understand that, you will run off and try to build yourself a fortune. The main point should be about doing the work of the Lord. David donated the best resources available in the world to build the temple. Nothing was too extravagant for the work of the Lord.

> Moreover there are workmen with thee in abundance, hewers and workers of stone and timber, and all manner of cunning men for every manner of work. (1 Chronicles 22:15).

David provided timber in abundance to build the temple. We often do not think of these things as money. David had to spend his money or wealth to obtain this timber. Wood costs money today. If you build a church or a television station, the materials cost money. Most ministry projects involve money. Money is important if we are going to fulfill the will of God and do the work of the ministry of Jesus Christ.

Jesus Himself said the fields are ready for the harvest

and to pray for laborers (Luke 10:2). We need laborers in the work of the ministry. How are those laborers going to live? How are you going to hire those laborers? How are you going to pay those laborers? How are you going to grow? How are you going to do anything? You need money to pay for almost everything you do.

God has everything you need. He has the resources available to help you accomplish what needs to be done to fulfill His calling and purpose for your life.

David gave $45 billion worth of gold and silver from his own personal wealth and he still had plenty to take care of his needs. You do not have to worry about yourself. When God blesses you with wealth, He gives you enough to accomplish His purpose and leaves enough left over to take care of your needs.

The more you give to God, the more He makes available to you. This is a spiritual law. This is the law of seed-time and harvest, sowing and reaping, giving and receiving. If you are generous toward God, He will make sure you always have more than enough to give to every good work (2 Corinthians 9:8).

"No more limits" applies to the finances you need to do what God wants you to do. There are no more limits on your finances. This is hard to understand, but you must try. You must dig into this until you understand it. You need to enter into the abundance of God for your finances so you will be able to give to the work of God.

The Unlimited Nature of God

It is difficult to understand the limitless nature of God. It takes time to reprogram our minds and eliminate the many misconceptions we have about God. I have heard people say, "You never know what God is going to

120

do. Sometimes He will bless you and other times He will not." These people are limited in their understanding of God. They are blind to the promises in the Bible. The Bible has been given to us to equip us for service and to guide us through the difficulties in life.

> **All scripture is given by inspiration of God, and is profitable for doctrine, for reproof, for correction, for instruction in righteousness: That the man of God may be perfect, thoroughly furnished unto all good works.   (2 Timothy 3:16-17).**

We are to use the Bible for our doctrine and to keep us in line with what God has in mind for us. God wants us to be corrected from our misunderstandings about Him so that we can be profitable in His service. The result of understanding the will of God in our lives is a life that is dedicated to doing good works for others. God's priority is to help others. We must always keep that in mind when we are trying to understand what God wants us to do. God wants to give us the resources we need to accomplish his purpose of helping people.

> **Now unto him that is able to do exceeding abundantly above all that we ask or think, according to the power that worketh in us,**
> **   (Ephesians 3:20).**

God has given us this wonderful promise to help us to take the limits off our minds. He wants us to understand he is not holding back anything. God has always had a priority of helping people. Many people have misunderstood the purpose of being blessed. God wants us blessed so that we can be a blessing. He wants us to abound in all areas of our life so we can help others.

Do we really grasp the meaning of *exceeding abundantly above all that we ask or think*? God is so much bigger and more powerful than we will ever imagine. We need to realize that no matter how big our problems seem to us, in comparison to what God is able to do, God's resources will always be more than enough for the task at hand.

Brainwashed with the Word of God

We have been "brainwashed." We have had our brains washed with the wrong solution. We have been programmed to be selfish. Our thoughts have been limited to what we can receive for ourselves. This is not a proper motivation. The proper motivation is for us to understand the love of God and to respond to this love in a way which blesses the world.

We need to be "brainwashed" with the word of God. You have to have your mind washed with the water of the Word. It's the water of the Word that's going to change you. It is going to change the way you think, the way you believe, the way you talk. It is going to change the way you walk and the way you live.

Paul said Jesus loved the church and gave Himself for it. He also said Jesus washed the church with the water of the Word of God.

> That he might sanctify and cleanse it with the washing of water by the word, That he might present it to himself a glorious church, not having spot, or wrinkle, or any such thing; but that it should be holy and without blemish.
>
> (Ephesians 5:25-27).

God wants us to grab onto His promises. We need to be cleansed by the word of God so we can understand His promises to us. God is not limited. We are the ones who are limited. God wants us to cleanse our bodies and minds so that we can be ready and able to serve Him and to serve a messed up world. Our mission is to reach lost and hurting people in the world and to tell them of the Good News of what Jesus has done for them. When we really understand what God has done for us through Jesus, then we will be more effective in reaching others.

God does not want us to be limited in helping others to find out about His goodness. God wants us to be equipped to do many good works. He does not want us to be limited by what we think. This is why it is important to read and study the Bible. The Bible renews our minds so we can understand the unlimited power and nature of God. God does not want us to be ignorant of His will for us. He has given us the Bible so we can understand what He wants from us.

God wants you to serve Him with all that is within you. He wants you to be pure and holy and separated from the ways of the world. He wants you to serve Him and obey Him. You start your service by dedicating yourself to understand and to put into practice the principles outlined in the Bible.

Paul summed up this dedication to serving God eloquently:

> I beseech you therefore, brethren, by the mercies of God, that ye present your bodies a living sacrifice, holy, acceptable unto God, which is your reasonable service. And be not conformed to this world: but be ye transformed by the renewing of your mind, that ye may prove what is that good, and acceptable, and perfect, will of God.
>
> (Romans 12:1-2).

Many minds are locked up to the limitless nature of God. The world is always struggling against God. The devil is the god of this world. He has spun many webs of deceit, which have sidetracked many people from understanding the true nature and goodness of God.

The worldly-minded Christian will never understand the limitless nature of God. A person bound by the limits of worthless religious traditions will never fully experience the limitless nature of God. Experiencing the limitless nature of God comes after dedicating oneself to serving God. Experiencing the limitless nature of God comes after your mind is renewed to the truth of the Bible, and after you are successful in applying its principles to your circumstances. However, changing and renewing your mind is a process that takes time. It takes time to grasp the unlimited nature of God and his willingness to bless you exceeding, abundantly, above all you can ask or think.

It Takes Time to Understand No More Limits

I have taught people for years about the promises in the Bible. I have had people come up to me, and I can tell by the way they talk to me or ask me a question that they do not understand what I have been saying. They have listened to me for years and they still do not understand how to apply what I am saying to their circumstances. It takes a while for some people to understand new ideas and principles. I am not being critical of these people, I am just saying it takes some people longer than others to learn things.

It took me two years to finish college algebra that is only a one-year course. It took me two years to pass it and even after I passed it, I did not understand it. I was glad when I finally finished that class. Statistics was another course that I had a hard time understanding. I was a psychology major at one time and had to take statistics. The head of the Psychology Department was the one that taught that class. I thought I was in a foreign country. I thought he must have been talking another language — random sampling, statistical information. Just thinking about these terms reminds me of how uncomfortable this was for me years ago.

My point is you can go to class and even pass, but do you really know anything about what you have been studying? The Word of God is like this to many people. They go to church and hear, but they do not understand what they hear. People hear things all the time and never put them into practice. The Word of God has to be put into practice if it is going to benefit you or those around you.

Do Not Wait for a Crisis to Dig into the Bible

You have to study and dig into the Bible for yourself. You have to dig to understand no more limits. Most people do not have any desire to dig into their Bibles until they find themselves in a crisis. Once in the crisis, they are motivated to dig into their Bibles to learn what they need to know to survive.

The St. Bernard and the Beagles

I remember when we had a St. Bernard dog named Eric. My wife, Jeanne, brought him home as a puppy. He was a precious little ball of fur, but he grew to be 200 pounds. I thought that I would make a housedog out of him until I heard this gnawing sound in the middle of the night. I went into the living room and he had chewed the arm off our couch. He had chewed the leather off, the foam rubber, everything. He had also regurgitated it all over the floor and was gnawing into the wood. That was the last time he was in the house. After this, he went outside to live the rest of his life.

Our next door neighbor had beagle dogs that barked at everything. If the wind blew they barked; if a leaf fell they barked; they barked at everything. Eric would walk around our yard and these beagles would stick their noses through a knothole in the fence and bark at him. They would just bark and bark. Eric would become tired of this. He would walk up to them, stick his nose in that knothole and bark once with his powerful sounding bark. The beagles would scatter.

Our neighbor built dog pens for his beagles. One of the dog pens was next to the fence. One day one of these little beagles wanted to see what was on the other side of the fence. He climbed on top of the dog pen next to the fence and jumped over into our yard. Here is our big St. Bernard lying there and all of a sudden he sees this little dog.

Eric stands up and lumbers over to investigate this little dog. This beagle sees this giant St. Bernard coming towards him. He panics and dives at the bottom of the fence and begins to dig and dig trying to return to his side of the fence. After he goes about half way under the fence, he becomes stuck. I can tell he thinks this big dog is coming after him, because he starts yelping and barking and digging with all four legs. He is doing all he can to go under that fence to return to where he belongs. He becomes stuck for a moment, but then he pushes himself through to the other side.

I share this story to say this: the only time some Christians dig for the things of God is when they are stuck under the fence and the devil's coming after them and their hind parts are sticking out. Then, they begin to dig into the Bible furiously because they are in a crisis. This is not the way it should be. You should dig into the Bible all the time. Every day you should be digging, digging, and digging some more to find out what God has promised you.

THERE ARE NO MORE LIMITS TO THE RICHES OF GOD'S GLORY
* * *

Paul's Prayer for You to Understand God's Love

Throughout this book I have quoted Ephesians 3:20. This Scripture is part of a prayer the Apostle Paul prayed for the believers in Ephesus. This prayer is as applicable to us today as it was to them. This is one of the most eloquent prayers in the Bible. Read the entire prayer and try to comprehend all that is being said.

> For this cause I bow my knees unto the Father of our Lord Jesus Christ, Of whom the whole family in heaven and earth is named, That he would grant you, according to the riches of his glory, to be strengthened with might by his Spirit in the inner man; That Christ may dwell in your hearts by faith; that ye, being rooted and grounded in love, May be able to comprehend with all saints what is the breadth, and length, and depth, and height; And to know the love of Christ, which passeth knowledge, that ye might be filled with all the fulness of God. Now unto him that is able to do exceeding abundantly above all that we ask or think, according to the power that worketh in us, Unto him be glory in the church by Christ Jesus throughout all ages, world without end. Amen.
> (Ephesians 3:14-21).

Paul prayed for the Ephesians to experience the love of God. Being rooted and grounded in the love of God makes living a victorious overcoming life possible. Love is the spiritual foundation for our faith. The fullness of God and the ability of God to do exceeding abundantly above all we can ask or think, are made possible by the love of God.

Paul prayed for us to comprehend the love of God. When you understand how much God loves you and wants to bless you it sets you free from the limits and boundaries that hinder you. Through understanding the love of God you can realize your potential through the power that works in your inner being.

God loves you as much as He loves anyone else. You do not have to be good enough or do anything to deserve His love. You must understand His love is what makes the benefits of an abundant life in Christ Jesus possible.

Because God loves you, there is no problem or situation that can arise which will be greater than the resources God has available to you. Once God's love is revealed to you, you will understand there are no more limits in God.

The Riches of God's Glory is Available to You

In the Ephesian prayer the Apostle Paul also uses the phrase "according to the riches of his glory" to describe how Christ could dwell in our hearts by faith. "According to the riches of his glory" we are grounded in love and obtain the fullness of God.

The Apostle Paul also used a phrase similar to "according to the riches of his glory" in the Ephesian prayer when he wrote his letter to the Philippians. He said to the Philippians:

But my God shall supply all your need according to his riches in glory by Christ Jesus.
(Philippians 4:19).

When Paul talks about the riches of God's glory, he is using this to tell us that there are no limits to what God can do. God can give you the ability to understand His love by the riches of His glory. God can let you know His fullness by the riches of His glory, and God can supply your needs by the riches of His glory.

The riches of God's glory are unlimited. There is no limit to what God can do for you spiritually, physically or financially through the riches of His glory. There is no limit that cannot be broken by the power of God's glory working in you through Christ Jesus. Nothing is too hard for God. There is not a single area of your life where there is a need that cannot be met by the riches of God's glory.

God has unlimited resources available to meet all your needs. Renew your mind to what the word of God says. Realize the riches of God's glory make the unlimited resources of God available to you. There are no more limits to the resources of God!

WHOEVER IS BORN OF GOD OVERCOMES THE WORLD

THE UNSEEN WORLD
AND ITS LIMITS
* * *

We live in a fallen world. There are spiritual forces that control the events of our lives. We cannot see electricity, but we can see its effects. We cannot see the devil, but we can see the results of evil in the world. People are killed by wars. Drunk drivers kill people. Innocent children die from cancer. Many things in this world point to an evil force.

We have already discussed in Chapter 4 how God is good and does not use evil to tempt His children (James 1:13). Satan is the god of this world. (2 Corinthians 4:4). Satan is the spirit behind crime, destruction and death. (John 10:10). Jesus is the force behind life and all that is good. (John 3:16).

The evil in the world cannot defeat a faith-filled Christian. The Apostle John wrote about how our faith in God brings victory over the world when he said:

> **For whatsoever is born of God overcometh the world: and this is the victory (nike) that overcometh the world, even our faith.** (1 John 5:4).

The limits of this world are imposed upon us by the evil world in which we live. We are in the world system but not of the world (John 17:16). We have to exist here, but we are not to be limited by the powers of darkness in control of the world system. We are to operate without limits in this world by the power of God. We are more than conquerors and triumphant over the world through Christ.

To better understand how we can overcome the limits of the world, let us look behind the scenes and examine the spiritual forces at work. The beginning of our struggle with evil began in the Garden of Eden. Adam and Eve sinned against God, and the human race was separated from God by their disobedience (Genesis 3:1-21). Jesus came into the world as a sinless man. He was the last Adam. Jesus never sinned, and He earned the right to redeem humanity from the power of darkness that came on the world when Adam and Eve disobeyed God. Jesus restored direct access to God. Jesus made it possible once again for people to experience the divine nature of God in their lives (Romans 5:1-21).

Adam and Eve Lost Dominion Over the World

Originally God created a world of order where everything was good (Genesis 1:1-31). God created a man named Adam and placed him in the Garden of Eden. The Garden of Eden was a beautiful paradise. Adam was given dominion over the world and all the animals, birds and fish. God and Adam walked together in the beautiful garden during the cool of the day. Adam was able to communicate directly with God and had fellowship with Him daily. God created Eve from Adam's rib so he would not be alone. All of Adam and Eve's needs were provided for abundantly by God. Man and woman lived in a place of perfect serenity and peace, the Garden of Eden. They did not have to work or toil. Pain, sickness, suffering and death were unknown. God's will was done on earth as it was in heaven (Genesis 2:1-25).

This picture perfect setting did not last long. There is a spiritual outlaw in the universe, the devil. He is subtle and crafty. He does not immediately make his presence known but operates cunningly behind the scenes. The devil came into this picture of perfection with a plan to steal, kill and destroy. The devil disguised himself in the form of what must have been at that time a beautiful creature, a serpent. Eve was walking in the garden and this beautiful creature began to talk to this innocent woman (Genesis 3:1-5).

God had placed two special trees in the Garden of Eden. There was the tree of the knowledge of good and evil and the tree of life. God had told Adam he could eat of any tree in the garden except the tree of the knowledge of good and evil. God said when you eat of this tree you will surely die (Genesis 2:17). The serpent succeeded in tempting Eve to disobey God. She fell for his trickery and ate of the forbidden tree. She gave the fruit to her husband and he ate as well.

The result of their disobedience was sin and they immediately lost their innocence. The consequences of their decision have affected all of us from that time to today. God banished Adam and Eve from the Garden of Eden to prevent them from eating of the tree of life and living forever with a spiritually dead nature. (Genesis 3:22-23).

Adam and Eve lost their paradise and experienced hardship, suffering and death. They lost their right to have dominion over the earth and the animals. They had to work and toil to survive. As a consequence of their actions, sin entered into the world and the world has been in turmoil ever since.

Jesus Regained Dominion Over the World

God was not done with humanity. He had a plan to buy us back or redeem us from our sins. The Bible is the story of God's plan to redeem humanity. Jesus is the cornerstone of God's plan of redemption (Luke 20:17). God sent His perfect Son to die for an imperfect world. Jesus' death on the cross paid the penalty for our sins. Through Jesus we are set free from the power of sin and the power of the devil (Acts 26:13-23).

The first Adam failed the test of the devil. Jesus, the last Adam, passed the temptations and tests of the devil. Jesus' death made it possible for us to again have direct access to the Father. Jesus' victory over death was a triumph over all evil. Jesus has made it possible for us to share in His triumph over the evil in the world (2 Corinthians 2:14).

Before Jesus was about to be crucified and die on the cross, He prayed for His followers to be kept from the evil in the world.

> I pray not that thou shouldest take them out of the world, but that thou shouldest keep them from the evil. (John 17:15).

God has a plan for His children. He wants us to remain in the world to do His bidding. Eventually, Jesus will return to restore the earth to the peace and harmony that existed in the Garden of Eden. He has promised He would return. However, until Jesus returns, we are expected to do great deeds in His name and to bring Him glory.

Jesus last words to His disciples were instructions to them to go and take His message to the world. He told them He had been given authority and dominion over heaven and earth. Jesus is in charge of the universe. Jesus has given us His authority to carry out His plan for the world. He wants us to glorify His Father in the world and to demonstrate the defeat of the devil.

> And Jesus came and spake unto them, saying, All power is given unto me in heaven and in earth. Go ye therefore, and teach all nations, baptizing them in the name of the Father, and of the Son, and of the Holy Ghost: Teaching them to observe all things whatsoever I have commanded you: and, lo, I am with you alway, even unto the end of the world. Amen. (Matthew 28:18-20).

Whoever is Born of God Overcomes the World

The great Apostle John talked about overcoming the world. He said if we were born of God that we could overcome the world.

> For whatsoever is born of God overcometh the world: and this is the victory that overcometh the world, even our faith. (1 John 5:4).

The word "world" used by John comes from the Greek word "kosmos." "Kosmos" can mean *planet*, or it can refer to the *world of darkness*. The evil world of darkness stands in opposition to the Kingdom of God.

When Adam sinned, he gave up his authority to Satan. Satan became god of this world (2 Corinthians 4:4). Jesus

135

has taken away the power of the god of this world. However, the god of this world continues to keep most people in darkness by his lies. Jesus came as the light of the world, and He has sent us out to share this light with those who are in darkness (John 12:46, Matthew 5:14). We are sent to proclaim truth to those who are in darkness. We are sent to free them from the kingdom of darkness and to spread the Good News of the coming kingdom of God (Acts 26:18).

Paul acknowledged the power of darkness. In Ephesians he said we struggle against evil spiritual forces.

> For we wrestle not against flesh and blood, but against principalities, against powers, against the rulers of the darkness of this world, against spiritual wickedness in high places.
>
> (Ephesians 6:12).

The word in the original Greek for "rulers of the darkness" is the word "kosmokrator." This word in Greek means *world ruler*. This reference to the world ruler of darkness is a reference to Satan.

Paul also painted a picture of a spiritual soldier doing battle against the rulers and powers of darkness. (Ephesians 6:13-18). This world of darkness is out there, but God has equipped us with all that we need to live victoriously and to overcome the darkness.

Jesus conquered Satan and destroyed his ability to deceive. Jesus has given us the ability to operate in victory, in success, to be an overcomer in a chaotic world. When you are born of God, you have the potential to be victorious and to overcome all the powers of darkness in this world.

Circumstances in the world can be overcome. If a doctor uses science to measure the limitations of your body and he finds cancer, disease or sickness, you can go to the Word of God and find that you can overcome it.

The circumstances of the world may limit you, but this does not mean they cannot be changed. The world sets limits on you, but you can move the perimeters. You can overcome your limits with the help of God.

We set boundaries for ourselves, or we let others set them for us. This is a practice we need to quit. We need to quit setting limitations, and we need to quit letting other people set limits on us that are contrary to the will of God.

Be of Good Cheer, Jesus Overcame the Limits of the World

Jesus overcame the limits of the world. He told his disciples he was an overcomer. He told them this so that they would have joy. He did not say they would not have problems. He said they would have problems in the world. He said they could find peace and joy in Him because He had overcome the world.

 These things I have spoken unto you, that in me ye might have peace. In the world ye shall have tribulation: but be of good cheer; I have overcome the world. (John 16:33).

It is easy for us to see Jesus as an overcomer. It is sometimes hard to see ourselves as overcomers. All of us have failed to live up to our fullest potential. However, our present situation does not mean the Word of God is not true. John said in 1 John 5:4, "Whoever is born of God overcomes the world." If you are a Christian you have the ability within you to overcome the power of the world and the limits of the world.

Greater is He That Is You than He that is in the World

John also stated you have the greatness of the Holy Spirit in you. This power from within gives you the ability to overcome the world and its limits. In the Apostle John's day there were some false prophets who were bothering some of his spiritual children (1 John 4:1-6). They apparently struggled against these false teachers and won a victory in their lives. The Apostle John said to them after their triumph of faith:

> Ye are of God, little children, and have overcome them: because greater is he that is in you, than he that is in the world.   `(1 John 4:4).

God has given us the Holy Spirit to guide us and to help us discern good from evil. When we follow the inner leading and urging of the Holy Spirit, we will fulfill God's will for our lives and bring glory to God (John 16:5-15). All Christians have this power within them. This power needs to be recognized and applied to all our situations and circumstances. The Holy Spirit gives us power over the limits of the world.

Jesus overcame the world and we can be full of joy because He defeated the evil God of this world. We have the right to enjoy the benefits of His victory over the devil. The strength and power of God are within in us, and we can be victorious over any limits the world of darkness can throw at us.

You Have the Right to Use Jesus' Name to Overcome Limits

The Bible is full of amazing promises. We have to go out of our way to *misunderstand* what it says. Jesus spoke plainly to His disciples before He went to the cross to be crucified. He gave His disciples instructions to carry on His work. Jesus expanded the limits of the work of the disciples.

> Verily, verily, I say unto you, He that believeth on me, the works that I do shall he do also; and greater works than these shall he do; because I go unto my Father. And whatsoever ye shall ask in my name, that will I do, that the Father may be glorified in the Son. If ye shall ask any thing in my name, I will do it. (John 14:12-14).

Religious tradition says we are no longer in the age of miracles. Miraculous works were only for a limited time. Miracles are no longer available today. With talk like this, some men will try to explain away Jesus' words to his disciples. Some men will go out of their way to try to prove with many arguments why the words of Jesus are no longer true today. They all agree they were true when Jesus was here, but they are not for us today.

Jesus' words *do* apply to us today. Jesus never intended for his works to stop with the death of the disciples. In fact, church history records many miracles and signs throughout the centuries since the time of Christ. Even today there are many documented reports of miracles occurring around the world. The writer of the letter to the Hebrews says:

> Jesus Christ the same yesterday, and to day, and for ever. (Hebrews 13:8).

Jesus taught His disciples to teach others what He had taught them. Jesus laid down the principles and He expected them to teach those who were to follow. Read the following words of Jesus again. As you read it realize, as a believer in Jesus, these words apply to you.

Verily, verily, I say unto you, He that believeth on me, the works that I do shall he do also; and greater works than these shall he do; because I go unto my Father. And whatsoever ye shall ask in my name, that will I do, that the Father may be glorified in the Son. If ye shall ask any thing in my name, I will do it. (John 14:12-14).

Do you believe in Jesus? Do you believe He spoke these words to all who believe in him? Then do not believe the nonsense of those who say these words no longer mean what they say. If you believe on Jesus, the works that He did you can do also. Jesus promises that you can ask anything in His name, and He will do it, so that the Father will be glorified in Him.

Jesus left us the power of His name. That is why you can stand in the face of sickness, disease, poverty and devils. At the sound of the wonderful name of Jesus in the mouth of a believer sickness, disease, lack and devils must flee.

Let this mind be in you, which was also in Christ Jesus: Who, being in the form of God, thought it not robbery to be equal with God: But made himself of no reputation, and took upon him the form of a servant, and was made in the likeness of men: And being found in fashion as a man, he humbled himself, and became obedient unto death, even the death of the cross. Wherefore God also hath highly exalted him, and given him a name which is above every name: That at the name of Jesus every knee should bow, of things in heaven, and things in earth, and things under the earth; And that every tongue should confess that Jesus Christ is Lord, to the glory of God the Father. (Philippians 2:5-11).

Everything that has a name must bow on its knees to

the name of Jesus. The name of cancer has to bow its knee to Jesus. Heart disease has to bow its name to Jesus. Poverty and lack has to bow its name to Jesus. At the sound of the name of Jesus everything must bow.

The name of Jesus has been given to the believer to do great and mighty works. There is no power on earth or in heaven that can stand against the power of the name of Jesus. There is no limit that can stand against the name of Jesus. All power in heaven and earth has been given to Jesus, and He has given us the right to use His name to the glory of God. The name of Jesus is a potent force for overcoming limits in our lives.

The name of Jesus is still as powerful and effective today as it was in the days of the early church. As a believer you have the right to use the name of Jesus to break through any barriers and expand the scope of Jesus' ministry to those around you.

The Least in the Kingdom of Heaven is Great In God's Eyes

When you accept Jesus Christ as Lord of your life you become a member of a spiritual kingdom, the kingdom of heaven. You have rights and privileges that are granted to you above and beyond what you can understand or imagine.

Jesus had some wonderful things to say about those who are least in the kingdom of God. He said the least person in the kingdom of God is greater than any person ever born.

> Verily I say unto you, Among them that are born of women there hath not risen a greater than John the Baptist: notwithstanding he that is least in the kingdom of heaven is greater than he.
>
> (Matthew 11:11).

This verse in Matthew said the least in the Kingdom of heaven is greater than John the Baptist, one of the greatest people ever born. How could that be? Let us go back to a couple of verses we have seen before.

> Nay, in all these things we are more than conquerors through him that loved us. (Romans 8:37).

> I can do all things through Christ which strengtheneth me. (Philippians 4:13).

Through the work of Jesus Christ, Christians can operate without limits as far as the will of God is concerned. God has not held back anything from you. God wants you to take advantage of your rights in the Kingdom of God to glorify Him in the world.

Keep Your Priorities Straight

It is important that you have proper priorities. The fact that you can overcome limits is not the most important thing in life. You need to overcome your limits, but the most important thing in this life is to have a loving relationship with Jesus Christ and to share that love with others.

The Apostle Paul had a good word about priorities when he said:

> Yea doubtless, and I count all things but loss for the excellency of the knowledge of Christ Jesus my Lord: for whom I have suffered the loss of all things, and do count them but dung, that I may win Christ, (Philippians 3:8).

You have all these rights and privileges in Christ. God has provided you with all you need to live victoriously in this life. He has given you His power and authority, but none of this is as important as knowing Jesus as your Lord. Loving God and his Son Jesus are more important than anything else in life. Love should be the strongest force operating in your life.

> And Jesus answered him, The first of all the commandments is, Hear, O Israel; The Lord our God is one Lord: And thou shalt love the Lord thy God with all thy heart, and with all thy soul, and with all thy mind, and with all thy strength: this is the first commandment. And the second is like, namely this, Thou shalt love thy neighbour as thyself. There is none other commandment greater than these. (Mark 12:29-31).

Give Glory to God

The spiritual power given to a Christian is immeasurable. The power of God is available to you to destroy the limits of the world. This is a fantastic privilege. This power will enable you have many victories over the powers of darkness around you. However, when you see the devils fleeing at the name of Jesus and your limits being broken, do not rejoice because you have power over the devil. Rejoice because your name is written in heaven.

> Behold, I give unto you power to tread on serpents and scorpions, and over all the power of the enemy: and nothing shall by any means hurt you. Notwithstanding in this rejoice not, that the spirits are subject unto you; but rather rejoice, because your names are written in heaven.
> (Luke 10:19-20).

We should not glory in the fact that the devil is subject to us. We should not glory in the fact we are superior to the forces of evil in the world. If we have anything we could glory in, it is in the glory of Jesus. The only thing worth glorifying in is the death and triumph of Jesus on the cross.

> But God forbid that I should glory, save in the
> cross of our Lord Jesus Christ, by whom the world
> is crucified unto me, and I unto the world.
>
> (Galatians 6:14).

The power and authority of the Apostle Paul put it all in perspective with these words. We should not glory in our authority over evil. We should not glory in our ability to overcome our limits. We should not glory in anything in the world. Our only glory should be in the Savior of the world, Jesus. Let everything be done for the glory of God and His son Jesus!

HOW TO OVERCOME THE LIMITS OF THE WORLD

YOU ARE IN THE WORLD BUT YOU ARE NOT OF THE WORLD

* * *

The book of Revelation describes two ways to overcome the power of the world and the devil. You can overcome by the "blood of the lamb" and the "word of your testimony."

> **And they overcame him by the blood of the Lamb, and by the word of their testimony; and they loved not their lives unto the death. (Revelation 12:11).**

This Scripture gives you insight into living a life without limits. A life without limits is an overcoming victorious life. You overcome by understanding your redemption in Christ, and by understanding the importance of the words you speak, which is your testimony to the world.

Revelation speaks of the connection of the blood of Jesus to our redemption from the world and the power of darkness. When we are in heaven, we will hear praises being sung about Jesus' blood.

> **And they sung a new song, saying, Thou art worthy to take the book, and to open the seals**

thereof: for thou wast slain, and hast redeemed us
to God by thy blood out of every kindred, and
tongue, and people, and nation; (Revelation 5:9).

Jesus is the only One worthy to receive our praises. He is the One who died and redeemed us by His blood from the power of darkness. He will receive well-deserved praise and adoration from those of us he has redeemed from all the nations of the world.

The second part of Revelations 4:11 shows you how important it is to give the proper testimony in your life as to what Jesus has done for you. You can overcome the devil by the word of your testimony. Jesus said you would be accountable for every word you speak.

But I say unto you, That every idle word that
men shall speak, they shall give account thereof in
the day of judgment. For by thy words thou shalt
be justified, and by thy words thou shalt be condemned.   (Matthew 12:36-37).

Understanding how you overcome by the "blood of the lamb" and the "word of your testimony" will help you to further understand how you can overcome the limits of the world. You live in the world but you are not of the world. (John 17:14). Everything you can learn about overcoming the limits in the world will help you to walk in victory and triumph over your circumstances. God wants you to overcome and to throw off the limits that keep you from being all He wants you to be. The blood of Jesus and the words you speak are important keys to helping you walk in victory over the limits of the world.

Overcome the World by the Blood of Jesus

* * *

The Significance of Blood Sacrifices

Today, it seems unusual to be talking about the religious significance of blood. Blood sacrifices are no longer a part of everyday life. In the days of the Old Testament, blood sacrifices were better understood. God established blood sacrifices as a way for His people to pay for their sins. God's justice was satisfied when the blood of an innocent animal was shed and offered as a penalty for sin.

Not just any animal would do for a blood sacrifice. Only certain animals and birds were acceptable as blood sacrifices. God established certain laws and regulations for offering animal sacrifices and other offerings. God established the priesthood to tend to these sacrifices and offerings. In the Old Testament, God established strict guidelines for the way the priests could approach Him. Priests could not minister before God as they pleased. Priests could only approach God in certain ways prescribed by the Law of Moses. Priests died when they failed to follow God's commandments concerning sacrifices and offerings (Leviticus 9:1-2).

The Jewish nation had several major holidays that involved an elaborate series of feasts and blood sacrifices. One feast and blood sacrifice was known as the Passover. This holiday celebration remembered the Israelites' escape from slavery in Egypt. Right before they left Egypt, the Israelite families were commanded to sacrifice a lamb and to put its blood upon the doorframes of their homes.

God's judgment was going to come on all those who were living in Egypt who did not have the blood of the lamb smeared on their doorframes. A destroying angel was sent to kill the firstborn of all those who did not have lamb's blood around their doors. The destroying angel would pass over the houses with the blood around the doorframes and not kill anyone there. This is the significance of the Feast of Passover. God's judgment rested upon the Egyptians, but His judgment and wrath passed over the Israelites.

After all the firstborn of the Egyptians were killed, the Egyptians were more than ready to allow the Israelites to leave Egypt. When the Israelites left Egypt, the Egyptians gave them their gold, livestock and other wealth and hurriedly sent them on their way. God redeemed His chosen people from slavery in Egypt. They left Egypt blessed with silver and gold (Exodus 12:36). They took the wealth of the Egyptians, and they also obtained a promise of good health (Exodus 15:26).

God took the Israelites into the desert and miraculously provided for their needs. He made water to come from rocks. It rained food, manna, from heaven every day. Over two million people were sustained in a desert environment for forty years (Deuteronomy 2:7). During this time God spoke to their leader Moses and delivered His laws to them. God through Moses also established the procedures for blood sacrifices and holidays during this time.

The first five books of the Bible tell of the early history of Israel and the establishment of the Jewish religion. The Jewish nation and religion were essential in God's plan to redeem mankind from sin, sickness, disease and poverty. The salvation of Israel from slavery in Egypt was symbolic of God's redemption for the entire human race.

The shedding of animals' blood was the forerunner of the shedding of the blood of Jesus. The shedding of blood in the Old Testament points to the centerpiece of salvation in the New Testament, Jesus dying for the sins of the world on the cross.

The Importance of Blood Covenants

The Old Testament and the New Testament are based upon covenants between God and His people. A covenant is a very involved form of a contract. A marriage relationship is a covenant relationship. There is the legal aspect but there is much more as far as relationship is concerned.

Blood covenants were common throughout Old Testament times. Blood covenants were much like our present day treaties between nations. They helped establish allies and trading partners. People would enter into these covenant relationships with one another for trade or protection from common enemies. Blood covenants were common and well understood as ways to seal agreements in ancient times.

Some North American Indian tribes have a blood covenant ceremony where men become blood brothers. The ceremony involves the mixing of blood between the parties entering into the relationship. A cut on the arm or hand is made and the blood is allowed to flow together. Blood brothers are pledged to help one another in time of need and to share in each other's success.

Abram entered into a blood covenant with God. Abram sacrificed animals and birds. God spoke to Abram and promised him a child through his wife Sarai. God also promised him the Middle East would be given to his descendants (Genesis 15:1-18). To this day the Arabs and Jews in the Middle East trace their ancestry back to Abraham. The Jews trace their ancestry through Abraham's son

Isaac, and the Arabs trace their ancestry through Abraham's son, Ismael.

Later, God confirmed his blood covenant with Abram and commanded him to be circumcised along with every male in his household. Circumcision was another form of a blood covenant. At this time God changed Abram's name to Abraham and his wife's name from Sarai to Sarah (Genesis 17:1-27).

God established another blood covenant in the desert with Moses and the Israelites. The priesthood made daily blood sacrifices as part of this covenant. This blood covenant was based upon the law given to Moses (Exodus 19:1-24:18). God established this blood covenant and followed the customs of the day by pronouncing blessings and curses upon the covenant relationship. If Israel followed the blood covenant, they would thrive and prosper. If the blood covenant was disobeyed, they would be scattered into the surrounding nations and suffer persecution (Deuteronomy 27:1-30:20).

Later, God established another blood covenant with King David. He promised David he would produce an heir who would be a king who would endure forever (2 Samuel 7:1-29). King David was a descendent of Abraham and Jesus was a descendent from King David (Matthew 1:1-16). Jesus was born into a line of men who had established blood covenant relationships with God. He was born at a time when Israel offered daily blood sacrifices in the temple. Jesus came and fulfilled the blood covenant obligations of Abraham, Moses and David perfectly (Hebrews 10:1-18). Jesus was the fulfillment of all the blood covenant promises ever made by God to people of faith (Acts 13:31-32, Romans 4:13).

Jesus came and established a new blood covenant sealed with His blood which was shed for many (Luke 22:17-20). Our tradition of communion with bread and wine is symbolic of the new blood covenant Jesus established. The word for "testament" means _covenant_. The Old Testament is the old covenant, and the New Testament is the new covenant. The idea of the blood covenant is an important theme underlying the entire Bible.

Overcoming Limits by the Blood of the Lamb

When you accept Jesus as Lord, you are entering into a blood covenant relationship with Him. When you obey the commandments of God and love God, you will be blessed with the privileges of the new blood covenant. The blood of Jesus Christ seals our victory and triumph over limits. Jesus was known as the lamb which was slain for the sin of the world (John 1:29). Jesus was the final sacrifice. All the animal sacrifices under the old covenant were finalized with the one sacrifice of Jesus Christ (Hebrews 10:9-12).

The Apostle John made an important statement about our ability to overcome limits in the book of Revelation:

> *And they overcame him by the blood of the Lamb, and by the word of their testimony; and they loved not their lives unto the death.*
>
> *(Revelation 12:11).*

This statement about overcoming by the blood of the lamb was a reference to our redemption in Christ. Jesus paid the penalty for our sins and He fulfilled all the obligations of the old blood covenants (Romans 10:4).

Jesus Redeemed You from the Curse of the Law

The old blood covenant had blessing s and curses. Sickness, disease and poverty were part of the curses of the old blood covenant (Deuteronomy 28:15-68). Jesus death redeemed you from the curses of the old blood covenant.

> Christ hath redeemed us from the curse of the law, being made a curse for us: for it is written, Cursed is every one that hangeth on a tree: That the blessing of Abraham might come on the Gentiles through Jesus Christ; that we might receive the promise of the Spirit through faith.
>
> (Galatians 3:13-14).

The blessings are all that are left after Jesus has done away with the curses. We have rights and privileges under the new blood covenant that include the blessings of the law (Deuteronomy 28:1-14). These blessings of the law go far beyond spiritual blessings. These blessings involve health and prosperity. You cannot separate health and prosperity from the blessings of the Old Testament blood covenants. Salvation, health and prosperity were all part of the blood covenant package.

The blood covenant and the communion we take with wine and bread is to remind us Jesus has redeemed us from the power of the devil. Just like the Passover was celebrated by the Jews to commemorate their deliverance from slavery, we are to celebrate communion as a reminder that we have been redeemed from the powers of darkness. We have been redeemed from sickness, disease and poverty by the blood of Jesus.

Our redemption by Jesus' blood includes freedom from the bondage of the limits imposed by the devil. Satan comes to steal, kill and destroy, but we have been redeemed from his power. We have a powerful blood covenant relationship with Jesus. We stand in victory over the power of the enemy by the blood of the lamb.

Overcome the World by the Word of Your Testimony

* * *

There is a Price to Pay for Being an Overcomer

The Apostle John explained that victorious Christians overcame the devil by the blood of the Lamb, and by the word of their testimony. We have looked at what it means to be redeemed by the blood of the Lamb. Let us look at the second part of this scripture, overcoming the devil and the world by the word of your testimony.

> **And they overcame him by the blood of the Lamb, and by the word of their testimony; and they loved not their lives unto the death.**
> **(Revelation 12:11).**

This reference in Revelation refers to overcomers as people who were willing to give their lives for their testimony. Notice that at the end of this verse it says they "loved not their lives unto death."

How many Christians are willing to die for what they believe today? In the time the book of Revelation was written, if you were a follower of Jesus Christ, you put your life at risk. Today, some people are still killed for their faith. In some countries Christians have been beheaded for sharing their faith. Others have been harshly persecuted in communist countries for their Christian beliefs.

Today, most Christians living in modern free countries are not faced with intense persecution. However, the Bible says a time of great tribulation will come. During this time, people will be forced to make a decision. They will have to choose between serving Jesus or serving the antichrist. If they will not forsake Jesus and His words, they will face tremendous persecution. They will be unable to buy and sell without the mark of the antichrist (Revelation 13:7). They will face hunger, thirst, scorching sun and death (Revelation 7:9-17).

Are you willing to risk your life for your Christian testimony? Are you willing to die for what you believe? There is a price to be paid for being a Christian. Do you really want to be an overcomer? Is the cost too much to bear? How willing are you to share your testimony and faith with others?

You can overcome the world by being a witness to what Jesus has done. You have to act upon Jesus' words and be obedient to the calling of God on your life. This is what it takes to be an overcomer. You must speak God's words and be a living witness of His grace and glory. You must not be ashamed of Jesus. Jesus left a solemn warning to those who would be ashamed of Him and His words.

> **For whosoever shall be ashamed of me and of my words, of him shall the Son of man be ashamed, when he shall come in his own glory, and in his Father's, and of the holy angels.**
>
> **(Luke 9:26).**

There is power in sharing the good news of Jesus with others. There is power in speaking the Word of God over your life and the lives of others. The Apostle Paul said he was not ashamed to give testimony about Jesus. Everywhere the Apostle Paul went he preached and taught about the power of Jesus Christ. His message was preached boldly. He was willing to suffer and die if necessary for what he believed.

> **For I am not ashamed of the gospel of Christ: for it is the power of God unto salvation to every one that believeth; to the Jew first, and also to the Greek.** **(Romans 1:16).**

The Apostle Paul was an overcomer. He overcame the devil by the blood of the lamb and the word of his testimony. He lived a life of faith and encouraged others to follow his example. He was stoned and left for dead, he was whipped, not once but five times. He was willing to pay a price for living a life without limits. He was willing to do whatever was necessary to be an overcomer and to bring glory to God.

The power to be a witness and to be an overcomer is available to you because you are redeemed by the blood of Jesus. In your weaknesses, God can strengthen you to be a witness and an overcomer. Jesus said His followers would receive power to be His witnesses in their city, their nation and throughout the earth.

> But ye shall receive power, after that the Holy Ghost is come upon you: and ye shall be witnesses unto me both in Jerusalem, and in all Judaea, and in Samaria, and unto the uttermost part of the earth. (Acts 1:8).

You should not be ashamed to speak up for Christ. You must be willing to stake your life on the Word of God and be a witness filled with the power of the Holy Spirit. This type of faith is the type of faith that will move mountains and overcome all the attacks of the devil.

Every Word You Speak Should Bring Glory to God

Jesus talked about the importance of every word you speak. The words you speak either justify you or condemn you. The words you speak should be chosen carefully to give glory to God. The words that you speak are your testimony. Does your testimony glorify God?

> But I say unto you, That every idle word that men shall speak, they shall give account thereof in the day of judgment. For by thy words thou shalt be justified, and by thy words thou shalt be condemned. (Matthew 12:36-37).

The words you use every day are part of your testimony. What is your testimony going to be? What words are you going to use? Are you going to speak the words of the world, or are you going to speak the words of God?

If the world says, "You are sick." Your testimony should be, "I am healed by the stripes of Jesus." (1 Peter 2:24).

If the world says, "You should worry about what you are going to eat or wear." Your testimony should be, "I will not worry about what I should eat or wear. I will seek first the Kingdom of God and these things will be given to me by my Heavenly Father." (Matthew 6:25-34).

If the world says, "You should live in fear." Your testimony should be, "I will not live in fear because God has not given me a spirit of fear; He has given me a spirit of power, love and a sound mind." (2 Timothy 1:7).

If the world says, "You are worthless." Your testimony should be, "I was bought with a price. I belong to God and I will glorify him." (1 Corinthians 6:20).

If the world says, "You are not forgiven." Your testimony should be, "My sins are forgiven and I am clean before God." (1 John 1:9).

Whatever the world throws at you, you can overcome by the blood of the Lamb and the word of your testimony. The Word of God is greater than any of your circumstances. Circumstances can be changed, but the Word of

God cannot be changed. Agree with the word of God rather than with your circumstances. Build your life on the solid rock of the faith-filled words of Jesus, not on the shifting sand of life's circumstances and feelings. If you believe the Word of God is true you will speak the Word of God out of your mouth. You either believe the Word of God is true or you believe your circumstances are true. When they do not agree, you should always believe the Word of God. That should be all there is to it.

THE BENEFITS OF OVERCOMING THE WORLD

* * *

Being an Overcomer Has Its Advantages

We have seen commercials in America which claim owning a particular charge card has its advantages. Owners of these cards are portrayed as having recognition and purchasing power. These cards are marketed in such a way as to appeal to people's pride. If you own one of these cards, the commercial implies, you will be seen as successful.

I can tell you that owning a charge card is not the key to a successful life. Being an overcomer in Jesus Christ is the key to a successful life! You have a heavenly account. God is keeping track of what you do with what He has given you. You will be rewarded for your works.

> **And, behold, I come quickly; and my reward is with me, to give every man according as his work shall be.** **(Revelation 22:12).**

Jesus is going to return soon. Jesus will come and judge the world. Those that do not believe in Him will be condemned. To those who do believe in Him, He will grant everlasting life. Those who believe in Him will receive the benefits of being an overcomer.

The Apostle John recorded the last words of Jesus in the last book of the Bible, Revelation. The book of Revelation was originally delivered to specific churches. These churches each received specific words from Jesus. Several times Jesus mentioned benefits that would be given to those who were overcomers. If you are a Christian, you are an overcomer. These promises are for you.

Eating from the Tree of Life

If you have ears, you need to listen to what Jesus is saying to the churches.

> He that hath an ear, let him hear what the Spirit saith unto the churches; To him that overcometh will I give to eat of the tree of life, which is in the midst of the paradise of God.
>
> (Revelation 2:7).

Two benefits of being an overcomer are that you will be in the paradise of God and you will eat of the tree of life.

There are no limits to what you can do with the help of God in your life. You can be an overcomer. When your life is over it will all be worthwhile. What we have in this life now is worthless when compared to knowing Jesus Christ and spending eternity with Him.

Spared from the Second Death

Those who are not overcomers will not be so fortunate. Those who do not know Jesus Christ as their Lord will be cast into a lake of fire. This is known as the second death. These unfortunate souls will face torment that was designed for fallen angels. Overcomers will escape this second death.

> He that hath an ear, let him hear what the Spirit saith unto the churches; He that overcometh shall not be hurt of the second death.
>
> (Revelation 2:11).

Secret Rewards

Jesus has some rewards that are hidden. You will be entitled to understand these hidden secrets. You will also receive a special stone with a new name known only by you and Jesus. You will not be just another face in heaven. Jesus will have a special name for you and only you.

> He that hath an ear, let him hear what the Spirit saith unto the churches; To him that overcometh will I give to eat of the hidden manna, and will give him a white stone, and in the stone a new name written, which no man knoweth saving he that receiveth it. (Revelation 2:17).

Power Over the Nations

A reward to overcomers is power over the nations. Many people today crave worldly power. Very few people have had power over nations. As an overcomer you will have this power. You, Jesus and other overcomers will rule and have more power and authority than any president, emperor, or king ever dreamed of having.

> And he that overcometh, and keepeth my works unto the end, to him will I give power over the nations: (Revelation 2:26).

More Blessings to Overcomers

Here are some more promises to overcomers. Your name will be written in the book of life and Jesus will announce you to His Father and the angels.

> He that overcometh, the same shall be clothed in white raiment; and I will not blot out his name out of the book of life, but I will confess his name before my Father, and before his angels.
> (Revelation 3:5).

159

Overcomers will be given a prominent place in the temple of God.

> Him that overcometh will I make a pillar in the temple of my God, and he shall go no more out: and I will write upon him the name of my God, and the name of the city of my God, which is new Jerusalem, which cometh down out of heaven from my God: and I will write upon him my new name. (Revelation 3:12).

Jesus will share His throne with overcomers. We will sit in the throne room and seat of power for the universe.

> To him that overcometh will I grant to sit with me in my throne, even as I also overcame, and am set down with my Father in his throne.
> (Revelation 3:21).

These promises are hard to imagine and believe. We are more than conquerors indeed. We will be given honor and power.

All this, however, is nothing compared to knowing and loving Jesus. We will all bow and worship Jesus, who is Lord of Lords and King of Kings. He is worthy to be worshipped and given all honor and power and glory forever.

Our time upon the earth is minuscule when compared to the eternity we will spend with Jesus. In Jesus Christ all Christians are overcomers. Being an overcomer is not an option. Make the most of the time you have in this life. Glorify God in everything you do.

You are an overcomer. You are triumphant in Christ. The greater one lives within you, and you have the power to overcome. The days of excuses are over; the days of limitation are over. Take your place as an overcomer. There are no limits in God. Go out and preach. Go out and win the lost. Go out and deliver the captives. Go out and set at liberty those that are bruised. You are an overcomer. Just do it!

FAITH IS VICTORIOUS OVER THE LIMITS OF THE WORLD

THE VICTORY OF FAITH

* * *

Faith Overcomes the Limits of the World

Throughout this book we have looked at what it means to overcome limits. In Chapter 1 we looked at the word for victory used in 1 John 5:4. We mentioned that the word for victory in the Greek is the word "nike."

> **For whatsoever is born of God overcometh the world: and this is the victory (nike) that over-cometh the world, even our faith.   (1 John 5:4).**

By faith we have victory in Jesus Christ. By faith we are made more than conquerors through Christ who loved us. (Romans 8:37). There are no circumstances in which we can be defeated when we serve God in faith. We will have trials of our faith but, if we endure with patience, we will have victory (James 1:2-4).

Victory over limits is accomplished by faith. In the last part of 1 John 5:4 it says, "the victory that overcometh the world, even our faith." Your victory over the evil in the world is obtained by faith. Faith is necessary to remove all the limits that grieve God in our lives.

You cannot remove limits in your life without faith. If you are going to remove limits in your personal life, your spiritual life, your physical life, your mental life or your emotional life, you must do it by faith.

FAITH CAN MOVE MOUNTAINS

* * *

Jesus Cursed A Fig Tree

Mark 11 describes how Jesus entered Jerusalem riding on a donkey. This was triumphant procession. Jesus was hailed as King of the Jews. People put palm branches in the road and cried out, "Hosanna! Blessed is he that comes in the name of the Lord!" (Mark 11:9). This was time of great rejoicing. After he entered Jerusalem that day, he left the city to spend the night in Bethany, just outside the gates.

The next morning Jesus was hungry. On his way into the city he passed by a fig tree and hoped to find some figs for breakfast. The tree had no fruit. Jesus said to the tree, "No man eat fruit of thee hereafter for ever." (Mark 11:14). The disciples who were traveling with him heard him speak to this tree. Jesus went on to clear the temple of moneychangers and to rebuke them for robbing the people. He finished His work for the day and went back to Bethany for the evening.

The next day they passed by the fig tree that Jesus had cursed and it had withered by the roots. Peter remembered what Jesus had said to the tree and pointed this out to Jesus. Jesus used this example of talking to a tree to teach His disciples about faith and prayer.

Jesus went on to discuss how important it was to have faith in God. He told them that they could not only speak to fig trees, but that they could even speak to mountains and have them thrown into the sea if they had faith.

> And Jesus answering saith unto them, Have
> faith in God. For verily I say unto you, That
> whosoever shall say unto this mountain, Be thou

removed, and be thou cast into the sea; and shall not doubt in his heart, but shall believe that those things which he saith shall come to pass; he shall have whatsoever he saith. Therefore I say unto you, What things soever ye desire, when ye pray, believe that ye receive them, and ye shall have them. (Mark 11:22-24).

Faith Delivers a Tormented Young Man

Jesus taught His disciples the importance of faith. One day a man brought his son, who was having seizures and suffering greatly, to the disciples. The disciples could do nothing to help the young man. The father then took his son to Jesus. Jesus rebuked His disciples for their lack of faith. He then cured the young man. After he did this, the disciples asked him why they could not help the young man.

> And Jesus said unto them, Because of your unbelief: for verily I say unto you, If ye have faith as a grain of mustard seed, ye shall say unto this mountain, Remove hence to yonder place; and it shall remove; and nothing shall be impossible unto you. (Matthew 17:20).

Jesus explained to them the reason they failed to heal the young man was because of their unbelief. I am sure it was hard for the disciples to accept the fact it was unbelief that had limited them from healing the young man. Everyone likes to think they have great faith. Jesus said it was their lack of faith that had limited them from helping the young man.

The Word of God is the Seed of Faith that Overcomes Limits

Faith makes all things possible. Faith is a supernatural force that allowed Jesus to do the impossible. Jesus compared mountain-moving faith to a mustard seed. A mustard seed is a tiny seed. Jesus said faith is like a small seed. He also taught His disciples a parable, known as the parable of the sower (Mark 4:3-33).

In this parable a farmer went out and sowed his seed. Some of the seed fell on the path and was eaten by birds. Other seed fell on rocky soil, and because it could not grow deep roots, it withered in the sun. Others fell among thorns that grew along side it and choked it so it could not produce fruit. Other seed fell on good ground and was fruitful.

Jesus explained this parable to His disciples. He told them the farmer was sowing the Word of God. The Word is the seed for faith. Some people hear the Word and live a life of overcoming faith. Others hear the same Word and live a life of defeat.

The seed that was sown on the path represents the Word of God that is heard, but goes in one ear and out the other. Those on the path hear the Word, and Satan comes immediately to steal the Word. When Satan steals the Word before it has time to grow, no fruit can be produced.

Others hear the Word and begin to act upon it, but because they do not develop good roots, they fail to produce fruit. When you are not rooted and grounded in the word of God, your faith will fail when the heat is turned up. This is what happened to those on rocky soil. Jesus said they were easily offended when affliction or persecution attack them. These trials come to steal the Word, and if they are not rooted and grounded in faith and love, their faith will fail.

The people represented by thorny soil are those who hear the Word, but because they are filled with cares of the world, fail to produce fruit. People can become distracted by the need to acquire riches and things. The desire to acquire riches is deceitful and causes the loss of the seed of faith. Faith that overcomes the world is not a faith that is distracted by the things of the world. A person who has overcoming faith will not allow themselves to be side-tracked by the cares of living. They know God is their source for all good things, and they have faith that God will meet their needs.

In the parable of the sower, people with successful faith are those who take the Word of God into their hearts and let it produce fruit. The Word of God is the seed of faith that overcomes limits in your life. Faith is the victory that overcomes the world. Jesus has won the victory, but you must live a life of faith to produce fruit for God.

Faith, Like Fruit, Grows on Branches

The Apostle Paul listed faith as part of the fruit of the Holy Spirit. The Holy Spirit lives on the inside of every believer. As a believer begins to act in faith on the word of God the fruit of the Holy Spirit is produced.

> But the fruit of the Spirit is love, joy, peace, longsuffering, gentleness, goodness, faith, Meekness, temperance: against such there is no law.
> (Galatians 5:22-23).

Faith is part of the fruit of the Spirit of God. Fruit is a natural product of trees that are healthy. Healthy trees do not have to struggle to produce fruit in their season. Trees do not decide when and how to produce their fruit. Trees produce fruit when the season is right. The branches cannot produce fruit by themselves. The branches must depend upon the tree for everything. The tree produces the fruit through the branches. The branches can do nothing apart from the rest of the tree. Faith is produced in the life of a believer because the believer is part of the tree.

Faith is like a seed. The seed has the power to grow

and develop when given the proper conditions. Seeds grow into plants or trees and eventually produce fruit containing more seeds. Faith will grow and be fruitful when given the proper conditions.

Jesus compared Himself to a grapevine and called His followers the branches.

> I am the vine, ye are the branches: He that abideth in me, and I in him, the same bringeth forth much fruit: for without me ye can do nothing. If a man abide not in me, he is cast forth as a branch, and is withered; and men gather them, and cast them into the fire, and they are burned. If ye abide in me, and my words abide in you, ye shall ask what ye will, and it shall be done unto you. Herein is my Father glorified, that ye bear much fruit; so shall ye be my disciples.
>
> (John 15:5-8).

Jesus illustrated how important the main part of the vine is to the branches. If we live attached to the vine we will be fruitful and productive. If the branch is not alive, it will become withered. Withered branches are cut off and burned. Branches that are attached to the vine are alive, strong and fruitful. The branches have no power in themselves. The branches exist so that the fruit has a place to grow. The branches that are well connected to the vine will be fruitful.

Faith Comes from Hearing the Word of God

God has given each of us a measure of faith. Faith is not something that only a few people are entitled to have. Faith is given to everyone.

> For I say, through the grace given unto me, to every man that is among you, not to think of himself more highly than he ought to think; but to think soberly, according as God hath dealt to every man the measure of faith. (Romans 12:3).

166

God has a measure of faith for everyone. God gives you the seed of the Word of God. The Word of God produces faith in the heart of hearers.

The Difference between Rhema and Logos

The Greek word for "word" used in the following verse is "rhema."

> So then faith cometh by hearing, and hearing by the word (rhema) of God. (Romans 10:17).

There are two Greek words that are translated into the English as *word* in the New Testament. They are "rhema" and "logos." "Rhema" is *a declaration or a command*. "Logos" is used more often and implies *an idea or concept*.

Let us look at a few verses where these words are used and discover the nuances of meaning that are lost in the translation.

The word "rhema" is used for "word" in the following verses:

> But he answered and said, It is written, Man shall not live by bread alone, but by every word (rhema) that proceedeth out of the mouth of God.
> (Matthew 4:4).

> If ye abide in me, and my words (rhema) abide in you, ye shall ask what ye will, and it shall be done unto you.   (John 15:7).

> It is the spirit that quickeneth; the flesh profiteth nothing: the words (rhema) that I speak unto you, they are spirit, and they are life. (John 6:63).

Another time a Greek phrase containing the word "rhema" is translated as *nothing*. This is found in the book of Luke where the Angel is speaking to Mary about the fact that she was going to give birth to Jesus. The angel said,

> For with God nothing (no rhema thing) shall be impossible. (Luke 1:37).

167

When God declares something personally to someone, when God gives a "rhema" word to someone, if they receive it by faith, it will come to pass. Mary did not doubt the word that came to her. She received it and became the mother of Jesus.

The devil tried to tempt Jesus to turn rocks into bread (Matthew 4). Jesus was hungry because he had been fasting for 40 days. Jesus could have turned the rocks into bread to satisfy his hunger. He had turned water into wine; turning rocks into bread would have certainly been possible. However, He did not fall for the devil's trick. Jesus refused to act on the devil's words. He said He would only act on the "rhema" word from God. If Jesus did not hear God tell Him to turn the rocks into bread, He would not do it.

Jesus said his "rhema" provides life itself. "Rhema" is the Word that God speaks to our hearts for particular situations. God gives us his "rhema" to direct and guide our lives. This is different from the other Greek word for "word" which is "logos."

"Logos" is the most common Greek word translated as "word" in the New Testament. It occurs 330 times. "Rhema" only occurs 70 times. "Logos" is most often found in the phrase *word of the Lord* or *word of God*. The following verses use the Greek word "logos" for "word."

> In the beginning was the Word (logos), and the Word (logos) was with God, and the Word (logos) was God.   (John 1:1).

> The sower soweth the word (logos).
>   (Mark 4:14).

> Making the word (logos) of God of none effect through your tradition, which ye have delivered: and many such like things do ye.   (Mark 7:13).

Another derivative of "logos" is "logikos." "Logikos" is where our modern word "logic" comes from. "Logos" is *the idea or concept* of what someone has said. "Logikos" is used for "word" in the following verse.

As newborn babes, desire the sincere milk of the word (logikos), that ye may grow thereby: (1 Peter 2:2).

The word "logos" can also mean *to account for something.* The word "account" in the following verse is "logos."

> And he called him, and said unto him, How is
> it that I hear this of thee? give an account (logos)
> of thy stewardship; for thou mayest be no longer
> steward.   (Luke 16:2).

In Revelation 12:11 the word of their testimony which overcomes the devil is the "logos." When you give an account of what God has done for you, this word defeats the enemy.

> And they overcame him by the blood of the
> Lamb, and by the word (logos) of their testimony;
> and they loved not their lives unto the death.
>   (Revelation 12:11).

The Word of God is both "rhema" and "logos." You should desire to study the "logos" of the Bible and to renew your mind with the "logos" of God. However, faith comes by hearing the "rhema" from God. The "rhema" of God is necessary to live in victory over your limits.

Faith begins when you hear the "rhema" of God in your heart. The Spirit of God lives in you, and as you become more familiar with the Bible, or the "logos" of God, it becomes alive in you. The Spirit of God activates the words of the Bible and they become the revealed Word of God to you, they become the "rhema" that you must live by.

The "rhema" is the life of God that comes from the vine and flows to the branches. The "rhema" of God is what will produce fruit in the branches. You can do nothing by yourself. It is the "rhema" of God that strengthens you and allows you to be able to do all things.

The "logos" says you are more than a conqueror. The "logos" says you are an overcomer. The "logos" says you can have no limits in what you can ask God. However it is the faith that comes from the "rhema" of God which allows us to be more than a conqueror and to triumph over our limits.

There is a difference between acting on a personal command of God and acting presumptuously. People can fall into trouble if they act on something they are not sure about. If you act without knowing the command of God, you can act presumptuously. Jesus told Peter to walk on the water. Peter had a "rhema" from God to walk on the water. If you do not have a "rhema" from God, do not try this on your own. You will sink. Do not presume because Jesus told Peter he could walk on the water you can walk on water.

Jesus had a "rhema" from God to put mud in a blind man's eyes to heal him (John 9:6). If you do not have a "rhema" from God to do this, it will not work. Peter had a "rhema" from God to command a lame man in the temple to rise and walk in the name of Jesus (Acts 3:6). Miracles are made possible by receiving a "rhema" from God.

Jesus said:

> If ye abide in me, and my words (rhema) abide
> in you, ye shall ask what ye will, and it shall be
> done unto you.   (John 15:7).

When the "rhema" abides in you, you can ask for whatever you need and it will be done for you. To know this "rhema" you have to abide in Jesus. To know this "rhema" you have to be sanctified by the "logos." To know the "rhema" from God, you have to spend time in prayer and in the Bible. When you know you have God's "rhema," you can shatter all limits. Nothing will be impossible when you hear the "rhema" of God and have faith.

LIMITS ON FAITH

* * *

Unbelief

Unbelief causes many to not receive from God. The Israelites were all eligible to receive blessings from God, but because of their unbelief they did not receive from God (Hebrews 3:17-19). Just because you are eligible does not mean you have faith to receive your blessings.

When Jesus visited his hometown, he was not accepted. He was unable to do miracles there. Matthew clearly tells why he could not do miracles in his hometown. It was because of their unbelief.

> And they were offended in him. But Jesus said unto them, A prophet is not without honour, save in his own country, and in his own house. And he did not many mighty works there because of their unbelief. (Matthew 13:57-58).

A passage from the book of Luke sheds a little more light on the situation.

> And he said, Verily I say unto you, No prophet is accepted in his own country. But I tell you of a truth, many widows were in Israel in the days of Elias, when the heaven was shut up three years and six months, when great famine was throughout all the land; But unto none of them was Elias

171

> sent, save unto Sarepta, a city of Sidon, unto a
> woman that was a widow. And many lepers were in
> Israel in the time of Eliseus the prophet; and none
> of them was cleansed, saving Naaman the Syrian.
> And all they in the synagogue, when they heard
> these things, were filled with wrath,
>
> (Luke 4:24-28).

Jesus reminded the people in His hometown about how God had sent the prophets Elijah and Elisha to a woman and a man from countries outside of Israel to bless them. God used the prophet Elijah to miraculously supply the widow's need for food by multiplying the last little bit of flour and oil she had (1 Kings 17:9-16). God brought Naaman the Syrian leper to the prophet Elisha to receive healing from his leprosy (2 Kings 5:1-20). There were many people in Israel who needed miracles, but God had to go outside the country to find people with faith. When Jesus said this, the people in his hometown became angry with him.

Unbelief kept people in Jesus' hometown from receiving financial blessings and healing. Jesus used the examples of the widow from Sidon and the Leper form Syria to illustrate this point. They had faith and received from God, but the folks in his hometown had unbelief and did not receive from God.

This situation is no different today. Many people are angry with God for not blessing them financially or healing their sick bodies. If you tell them it is because of their unbelief they will get angry with you. Unbelief is a limit in the lives of many Christians that keep them from receiving the blessings of God.

Sickness, disease and lack are still problems we face in the world everyday. Faith in God is the solution for overcoming these limits in our lives. Jesus came to teach us how to receive what we need from God by faith. Jesus did not limit God to meeting only spiritual needs. God can meet your physical and financial needs as well as your spiritual needs. God is willing to meet your physical and financial needs if you can overcome the limit of unbelief.

Unbelief

It is hard for many people to realize that unbelief is a limit, but unbelief keeps people from receiving the blessings of God. Many people today are offended when Jesus does not work miracles on their behalf. Ask yourself this question, "Could it be possible that Jesus can do no mighty works in our churches today because of unbelief?" The answer to this question is an emphatic "Yes!" Another good question to ask is, "If we had faith, could Jesus do mighty works in our churches today?" The answer to this is also an emphatic "Yes!"

fear
doubt

Fear and Doubt

Doubt is an enemy of faith and robs faith from its effectiveness.

> **Jesus answered and said unto them, Verily I say unto you, If ye have faith, and doubt not, ye shall not only do this which is done to the fig tree, but also if ye shall say unto this mountain, Be thou removed, and be thou cast into the sea; it shall be done.** (Matthew 21:21).

Doubt is different from unbelief. <u>Unbelief is denying the Word of God is true.</u> Doubt acknowledges the Word of God is true, <u>but it fails to believe the Word is true now for</u> a particular situation. Doubt says, "I am not sure the time is right. Maybe later, but not now." Faith is always in the present tense. Faith is something you have now. Faith says, "It is time to receive at this particular moment." Faith is being convinced God's words are truer than the negative circumstances. When the light of faith is in your heart, the darkness of fear disappears.

173

Fear and doubt go hand in hand. Fear is expecting the worst will happen. Fear is a wrong way of thinking and is also a strong emotion.

> And Peter answered him and said, Lord, if it be thou, bid me come unto thee on the water. And he said, Come. And when Peter was come down out of the ship, he walked on the water, to go to Jesus. But when he saw the wind boisterous, he was afraid; and beginning to sink, he cried, saying, Lord, save me. And immediately Jesus stretched forth his hand, and caught him, and said unto him, O thou of little faith, wherefore didst thou doubt?
> (Matthew 14:28-31).

Peter saw Jesus walking on the water and he wanted to walk on the water. Jesus commanded Peter to step out of the boat and he began to walk on the water. Peter looked around and saw the wind and the waves. He began to fear for his safety. He then began to doubt, and then he began to sink. Jesus reached out and steadied him, and then all his fear and doubt disappeared.

Fear and doubt limit you from receiving from God. Peter had a spoken "rhema" word from the Lord to walk on top of the lake, yet because of fear and doubt he began to sink. Fear and doubt keep us from believing the "rhema" word of the Lord, but with help from Jesus, we can overcome our fears and doubts. With the help of Jesus we can do mighty works.

We are so programmed to think about the worst things happening that we miss out on many miracles. God wants us to learn to overcome our fears and our doubts. He wants us to be people of great faith. Fear and doubt keep our faith small. God wants us to have unlimited faith. If we have faith instead of doubt and fear, we can move mountains. Victorious faith overcomes the limits of unbelief, fear and doubt.

Lack of Action

Faith requires corresponding actions. Faith is more than just talking. Faith is talking and doing.

> **For as the body without the spirit is dead, so faith without works is dead also.** (James 2:26).

Years ago, a man and his wife came to a meeting I had in another town. The wife was upset at her husband. The man said he was called into the ministry. The wife was upset because he would not work. She was working and paying all the bills. He said he was living by faith. She made him come up to the altar for prayer.

I asked what they wanted prayer for. The wife told me that he would not work. I asked him to tell me more about the situation. He said the Lord told him to start a ministry. I asked if he had started it, and he said he had not. It turns out he was not doing anything to prepare for the ministry. He was just sitting around the house watching TV and doing nothing productive.

I looked at the wife and told her to quit feeding him. I told him the Bible says, "If you do not work, you do not eat." I told her if she would quit cooking for him and feeding him, he would go to work. He did not like what I said and he left angry.

This man was not living in faith. He had no corresponding actions to go with his words. He said he was going to start a ministry, but he was not doing anything but being lazy. Faith without works is a dead faith. If you do not add actions to your faith, you are limited from being blessed by God.

Living by Faith Pleases God

God has pleasure in those who have faith and act on His promises. God is not pleased when you do not have faith.

> Now the just shall live by faith: but if any man draw back, my soul shall have no pleasure in him.
> (Hebrews 10:38).

God is pleased when you use your faith to break limits in your life. God rewards you for seeking Him and doing His will.

> But without faith it is impossible to please him: for he that cometh to God must believe that he is, and that he is a rewarder of them that diligently seek him. (Hebrews 11:6).

The writer of the book of Hebrews goes on in the next few of verses in Chapter 11 to talk about the faith, obedience and actions of heroes of the Bible. All these heroes overcame the limits of the world. Noah by faith built an ark and saved the human race from extinction. Abraham left his home country by faith and received many blessings from God. Sarah, Abraham's wife, conceived and had a child, which was a direct ancestor to Jesus. All these triumphs resulted from having faith in God. Their faith helps us to understand whatever is born of God overcomes the limits of the world, *and this is the victory, even our faith* (1 John 5:4).

CHAPTER 13

INCREASE BEYOND YOUR LIMITS

THERE IS NO LIMIT TO WHAT YOU CAN DO

* * *

Through the help of Christ, you can do all things.

I can do all things through Christ which strengtheneth me. (Philippians 4:13).

"All things" means there is no limit to what you can do. Even though you are weak in yourself, when you live by the power of God and faith, there is no limit to what you can do in Christ.

God has a wonderful plan for your life. He loves you and desires for you to return that love to Him. When you love God, you show this love by the actions in your life. There is more power inside the least Christian than you could ever imagine. There is no excuse for you not to glorify God with your life.

The purpose of this book is to help you throw off the limits that are keeping you from being all God wants you to be. Whatever state you are in physically, financially or spiritually, you can overcome your limits with the help of God. God has an unlimited plan for you. When you find the will of God for your life, you can increase beyond your limits.

No more limits is about entering into the fullness of God. No more limits means reaching beyond your current circumstances and tapping into the unlimited resources of God. No more limits means you are able to do all things through Christ who strengthens you. No more limits means finding out the will of God for your life and receiving the fullness of God's provision.

If you would be honest with yourself, you would realize there are some areas in your life where we have set limits where God is concerned. You have set boundaries for whatever reason. If you will allow the Holy Spirit to reveal them to you, He will show you these limits. God wants you to recognize your limits and go beyond them.

Extend Your Boundaries

God spoke to Israel about how He planned to enlarge the boundaries of their nation.

> **For I will cast out the nations before thee, and enlarge thy borders: neither shall any man desire thy land, when thou shalt go up to appear before the LORD thy God thrice in the year.**
>
> **(Exodus 34:24).**

He was talking about defeating the enemies of the nation of Israel and the principle at work here might apply to us. He said He was going to cast out those nations or those obstacles before them and enlarge their borders.

God promised the nation of Israel that if they followed His words, He would increase them beyond their limits. If you have faith in God's words, He will remove the obstacles before you. God wants to extend your boundaries. God will give you the ability to do more than you ever thought possible. The seed of faith in your heart will grow and you will steadily increase beyond your limits.

Three Ways to Increase Beyond Your Limits

We are going to look at three things in this Chapter that will help you increase beyond your limits. First, you can increase by setting goals. Goals help you reach beyond old limits and establish new parameters. Second, you can increase by the words you speak. The words you say either reinforce your old limits or they help you expand to new horizons. Third, you can increase by the actions you take. Actions determine how far you will go with the goals you set and the words you say. These three things are important in helping you to understand how to apply your faith to real life situations.

Increase by Setting Goals

If you do not know where you are going, how are you going to know if or when you reach your destination? Goals are important. We should set goals. The most important goal for Christians to pursue is our calling in God. The Apostle Paul said:

> **I press toward the mark for the prize of the high calling of God in Christ Jesus.**
>
> **(Philippians 3:14).**

The Apostle Paul set his sights on a marker in the distance farther ahead than where he was at the time, and he went toward it with great focus and determination. Your goal should be to know Jesus Christ and fulfill His plan for your life.

Have you ever been praying and all of a sudden you feel like your prayers are not going any higher than the ceiling? You do not feel like you are getting through to God. Then there are times you are praying and you think you are really making contact with heaven. This is when you know you are in His presence. You should want to enter into his presence every time you pray. If you are limited in your prayer life, you are going to be limited in the results.

You need to set goals where your prayer and spiritual life are concerned. The most important things you can do to help develop your spiritual life are to read your Bible and pray. Set goals to spend time in prayer and Bible study, and God will give you wisdom to know His will for your life.

Where do You Want to be 20 Years from Now?

Goal setting is important for all areas of your life. Goals are important in spiritual areas, but goals are important in other areas as well. For instance most people do not adequately plan for their retirement. They work for years and when they retire they have nothing to show for it. Unfortunately, too many people end up depending on someone else to support them during their golden years. Without extra money other than government checks many people live their golden years severely limited.

Even ants plan for their future. How much more should man, God's most precious creation, plan for his future.

> Go to the ant, thou sluggard; consider her ways, and be wise: Which having no guide, overseer, or ruler, Provideth her meat in the summer, and gathereth her food in the harvest. How long wilt thou sleep, O sluggard? when wilt thou arise out of thy sleep? Yet a little sleep, a little slumber, a little folding of the hands to sleep: So shall thy poverty come as one that travelleth, and thy want as an armed man. (Proverbs 6:6-11).

Where do you want to be 20 years from now? What kind of nest egg do you want to have saved by the time you retire from your job? What kind of method or plan do you need to accomplish your retirement goals? What do you want to have by the time you are 62 or 65?

The best time to start saving for your retirement is while you are younger. The older you become, the less time you have to properly save for retirement. If you can figure out what you need to retire, and if you can save towards that goal, that is good. If you can not, you need to pay someone to help you make a financial plan for your future.

Whatever you want to accomplish for your retirement is your mark or goal. You should set aside a certain amount each month now in order to accomplish your goals in later years. It may not seem like much now, but it will add up to a lot if you do this consistently year after year. The best time to start is early in your working career. The later you wait, the more you will have to put in to obtain your goals.

You can set goals in all areas of your life. Goals need to be measurable and realistic. Break the goal down into parts. Set major goals and develop minor goals to work towards your major goals. Setting a goal to make more money or to lose some weight is not specific enough. Set a goal to make a certain amount of money or to lose a certain amount of weight in a certain amount of time.

If you are 100 pounds overweight set a goal that is realistic. Do not try to lose 100 pounds in one month. Try to lose two pounds a week. Change your lifestyle and your eating habits to do this. This will bring long-term changes.

You should learn new skills and knowledge to help you meet your goals. You should take action immediately when you set a goal. You should not wait until all the lights are green to go downtown. This may never happen. You should start where you are today to take steps toward a new future.

If you already know how to set goals for your work, business or professional life, you should also set goals for your Christian life. Set goals for serving your local church. Set goals for whatever you want to do for God. Pray and ask for wisdom. God will show you what to do to please Him. God will give you the right steps to take.

You may be able to make many plans but the plan that will work best is the plan with the Lord's blessing. When you find his plan, you will be assured of success.

> **Trust in the LORD with all thine heart; and lean not unto thine own understanding. In all thy ways acknowledge him, and he shall direct thy paths.** (Proverbs 3:5-6).

Do you have problems with unforgiveness? Set a goal to overcome it. Do you have trouble with anger? Set a goal to overcome it. Do you an attitude of pride? Set a goal to overcome it. Do you have a problem with foul language? Set a goal to overcome it. Whatever is a limit in your life, you can set a goal to overcome that with the help of God.

Do you lack joy in your life? Are you dry spiritually? These are spiritual boundaries. Set goals to find joy and be watered spiritually. You may have to make some important changes in your life to accomplish your goals. Goals help you make successful changes. Goals help you move in the direction that you need to go. Goals help you make the necessary corrections to stay on the right course.

Goals help you fulfill the will of God in your life. If you are diligent in seeking God's will for your life, you will find it. If you are obedient to His word to you, your goals will be successful and you will fulfill God's plan for your life.

Learn to Prioritize Your Day

Goals make it easier to establish priorities. By establishing clearly defined goals, you can make decisions about what you are going to do with your time. You should look at your goals and decide every day to work towards those goals.

Everyone is in a different place in life. I am still learning how to use my time wisely. Time is one of the most precious commodities we have. Once a day is over, you can never have that time back. You should make the most of each day.

> **See then that ye walk circumspectly, not as fools, but as wise, Redeeming the time, because the days are evil. Wherefore be ye not unwise, but understanding what the will of the Lord is.**
> **(Ephesians 5:15-17).**

I have learned to prioritize my time. I have had to learn to prioritize my goals and projects. If you are not careful, you can lose a whole day and not accomplish important tasks because of distractions. It is Satan's job to distract us from doing the will of the Lord.

You have to set priorities on what is important to do each day. I carry a daily planner. I assign priorities to the things I need to accomplish. If I have ten things to do each day, I will assign one of three priorities: A, B or C. "A" is my top priority. I must do this today. "B" is important and needs to be done, but "B" is not the most urgent. "B's" can be done the next day, if they are not finished today. "C's" are things which should be done, but they can be done later if I do not finish all the "A's" and "B's."

This system works well in doing the work of the ministry, and it can be applied to other situations as well. If you are a working mom, a dad, a student, or whoever, you can plan your daily activities and set priorities.

How will you know when you have accomplished anything if you do not set goals? Setting up a mark in the distance or in the future helps you measure progress toward your goal. Setting goals help you know when you have done what you set out to do.

Goals and priorities involve taking risks. You risk failure whenever you set a goal. Every risk also carries with it a potential reward. The greatest risks usually return the greatest rewards. Goals help you determine what risks you want to take.

Increase by the Words You Speak

The second way to extend your boundaries is by the words that you speak. One important aspect of extending your boundaries is to change the way you speak.

God created the world with His words. God created man in His image and gave him the ability to speak words. Jesus said His words were spirit and life (John 6:63). Your words can be spirit and life as well. Your tongue is a little member, but it can bring much damage or bring much blessing. (James 3:5, Proverbs 13:2).

If you are going to increase beyond your limits and move into new areas, you must change the way you speak. When you speak the words and the language of God, you will increase beyond your limits.

God Created Language

God gave us the wonderful gift of communication. Words are containers of meaning. Without words, life as we know it would be impossible. Words allow us to talk to one another and to work together. Words are an essential part of life.

Different languages came into being miraculously. At one time everyone spoke the same language (Genesis 11:1). This ability caused sinful men to work together for the wrong reasons. God wanted the human race to expand beyond the limits of where they were living, but they were not willing to do so. God caused them to speak in different languages so they would go and settle in different areas of the world.

> And they said, Go to, let us build us a city and a tower, whose top may reach unto heaven; and let us make us a name, lest we be scattered abroad upon the face of the whole earth. And the LORD came down to see the city and the tower, which the children of men builded. And the LORD said, Behold, the people is one, and they have all one language; and this they begin to do: and now nothing will be restrained from them, which they have imagined to do. Go to, let us go down, and there confound their language, that they may not understand one another's speech. So the LORD scattered them abroad from thence upon the face of all the earth: and they left off to build the city. Therefore is the name of it called Babel; because the LORD did there confound the language of all the earth: and from thence did the LORD scatter them abroad upon the face of all the earth.
>
> (Genesis 11:4-9).

God had to change their words to cause them to expand beyond their limits. God had to change their language to keep them from doing what they had imagined to do. He said in Genesis 11:6, "nothing will be restrained from them." In other words, they can do whatever they want to do. Those ancient men were not building the Tower of Babel to glorify God. They were building the Tower of Babel to make a name for themselves. God changed their language and changed their plans to suit His purpose. When God changed their words, He changed the way they lived.

God also used different languages in the book of Acts to change people. Jesus' disciples were commanded to remain in Jerusalem until they received power from God to be his witnesses (Acts 1:8). God gave them a supernatural gift of languages that enabled them to communicate with people from all over the world. This was the reverse of what had happened at the Tower of Babel. God wanted Jesus' disciples to be understood by everyone in the world.

> And when the day of Pentecost was fully come, they were all with one accord in one place. And suddenly there came a sound from heaven as of a rushing mighty wind, and it filled all the house where they were sitting. And there appeared unto them cloven tongues like as of fire, and it sat upon each of them. And they were all filled with the Holy Ghost, and began to speak with other tongues, as the Spirit gave them utterance. And there were dwelling at Jerusalem Jews, devout men, out of every nation under heaven. Now when this was noised abroad, the multitude came together, and were confounded, because that every man heard them speak in his own language. And they were all amazed and marveled, saying one to another, Behold, are not all these which speak Galilaeans? And how hear we every man in our own tongue, wherein we were born? (Acts 2:1-8).

On the Jewish holiday of Pentecost, people had come to Jerusalem from all over the world. The disciples spoke in tongues, and all the people heard the Good News of Jesus preached to them in their native languages.

This was the birthday of the Church. When God gave the gift of speaking in unknown languages to the disciples, He changed the way they thought of themselves. They received supernatural power to be His witnesses throughout the world. When God changed the words they spoke, He changed the way they lived.

Even today, the Bible is translated into more languages than any other book that has been written. Bible translators are still working hard to make the Word of God available to all language groups in the world. Billions of people are now able to read and understand the Word of God in their own native language thanks to the work of thousands of dedicated missionaries who are translating the Bible. The ability to have the words of God available to us in our native language is a wonderful gift from God.

Change the Way You Live by Changing What You Say

The words of God are powerful. Your words can be powerful as well. One of the most solid obstacles in the world is a mountain. Mountains seem impossible to move. Jesus did not see anything as impossible. He said if we had faith, we could speak to a mountain and it would be moved. You must learn how to speak to your limits in faith.

For verily I say unto you, That whosoever shall say unto this mountain, Be thou removed, and be thou cast into the sea; and shall not doubt in his heart, but shall believe that those things which he saith shall come to pass; he shall have whatsoever he saith.   (Mark 11:23).

Jesus emphasized speaking to this mountain. He mentioned speaking to it three times in this verse. He said, "whosoever shall say unto this mountain." Then Jesus said, "believe those things which he saith." Then he said, "he shall have whatsoever he saith." Jesus intertwined faith and speaking to the mountain together. Speaking words and faith go hand in hand. You cannot have faith without speaking words of faith. Words are the containers that support your faith. Jesus pointed out that speaking to the mountain was an important part of having faith.

Words Come from Your Heart

Words come from your heart. What you believe is what you speak. Jesus said what is in your heart comes out in the words you speak.

> A good man out of the good treasure of his heart bringeth forth that which is good; and an evil man out of the evil treasure of his heart bringeth forth that which is evil: for of the abundance of the heart his mouth speaketh.   (Luke 6:45).

Faith comes when you hear God speak to you (Romans 10:17). The revelation of the Word of God to your heart causes you to speak faith-filled words. These faith-filled words set spiritual forces into operation.

God Created Everything by First Speaking Words

When God created the world He first said words. The story of creation in Genesis 1 is full of verses that demonstrate the power of God's words. Every day, whatever He said came to pass. God created the land and seas by first speaking words. He created plants and animals and man by speaking words. You and I are here today because God spoke words that came to pass.

188

Isaiah says every word God speaks is valuable and accomplishes something valuable.

> For as the rain cometh down, and the snow from heaven, and returneth not thither, but watereth the earth, and maketh it bring forth and bud, that it may give seed to the sower, and bread to the eater: So shall my word be that goeth forth out of my mouth: it shall not return unto me void, but it shall accomplish that which I please, and it shall prosper in the thing whereto I sent it.
>
> (Isaiah 55:10-11).

You Are Saved by the Words You Speak

Your words justify or condemn you. Faith-filled confession of the Lord Jesus brings salvation. Your confession of Jesus as Lord of your life changed your eternal destiny. You will live with Jesus forever and escape the fires of hell because of the words you spoke. The value of your words is priceless.

> That if thou shalt confess with thy mouth the Lord Jesus, and shalt believe in thine heart that God hath raised him from the dead, thou shalt be saved. For with the heart man believeth unto righteousness; and with the mouth confession is made unto salvation. (Romans 10:9-10).

Jesus said,

> For by thy words thou shalt be justified, and by thy words thou shalt be condemned.
>
> (Matthew 12:37).

Speak to Your Limits

You can speak to the limits in your life and tell them to be removed. If you have faith in God, and if you know His will for you, you can speak to limiting mountains and tell them to be thrown into the sea and they will be moved. Jesus said it was possible to move mountains by faith.

Jesus spoke to situations and circumstances and changed them. He spoke to a storm and calmed it (Mark 4:39). He spoke to a man who had been dead for days and he came to life (John 11:43). He spoke to people facing all kinds of adversities, and His words brought victory and triumph.

After Jesus spoke and instructed His disciples, His words and teachings changed the world forever. Follow Jesus Christ's example. Learn to speak the words of God in faith and you will smash your limits.

When lack tries to worry you, say, "My God supplies all my needs according to his riches in Glory!" (Philippians 4:19).

When sickness tries to overcome you, say, "I am healed by the stripes of Jesus!" (1 Peter 2:24).

When fear of disaster tries to unsettle your mind you can say, "God has not given me a spirit of fear. He has given me His love power and a sound mind!" (2 Timothy 1:7).

If Jesus' words live in us, we can speak His words back to God, and God will give us whatever we ask (John 15:7). Our words are valuable. Life and death are in the power of the tongue (Proverbs 18:21).

Increase by the Actions You Take

You can increase beyond your boundaries by the goals you set, by the words you speak, and by the actions you take. Faith requires corresponding actions to be a living faith. Faith without actions is a dead faith.

> Even so faith, if it hath not works, is dead,
> being alone. Yea, a man may say, Thou hast faith,
> and I have works: shew me thy faith without thy

> works, and I will shew thee my faith by my works.
> Thou believest that there is one God; thou doest
> well: the devils also believe, and tremble. But wilt
> thou know, O vain man, that faith without works is
> dead? (James 2:17-20).

Just because you believe there is a God does not mean you have done much. The devil and his cohorts believe there is a God too (James 2:19). You have to do more than believe that God is real. You have to put your faith into action.

I believed Jesus Christ was the Son of God all my life. That was what I was told. I knew this, but I did not act on it until I was almost 30 years old. I acted in faith after I heard a pastor preach the Word of God and tell me that I had to confess Jesus as my Lord and believe God raised Him from the dead. I had to walk down the aisle and say this with my mouth. When I stood in front of the preacher and said this, I became born again. I was saved. I believed Jesus was the Son of God all my life, but I never acted on it. After I acted on the Word of God, I received a new life in Christ Jesus.

It is a beautiful thing to watch people understand the idea of no more limits and put it into practice in their lives. People who put these principles into action will see results. People who only think about it briefly will never experience the fullness of God in their lives. The idea of no more limits in your life will only work if actions are taken.

Two Boats and a Helicopter

This story is about a man who is waiting for God to save him from a flood. The waters begin to rise. His street and yard become flooded with water. A neighbor comes by with a small boat and asks him if he needs help. The guy in the house says, "No I am waiting for God to save me."

The water continues to rise and the guy goes up to the second floor of his house. Another man comes by in a bigger boat and asks him if he wants help. The guy in the house says, "No, I am waiting for God to save me."

The water rises to the point where the man is on the roof. A helicopter comes by and the pilot asks him if he needs help. He tells the men in the helicopter he is waiting for God to save him. The helicopter flies away.

Finally, the flood washes the man off the roof and he drowns. He goes to heaven and stands before God and asks, "Why didn't you save me?"

God replies, "I sent you two boats and a helicopter! What else did you want?"

The moral of this story is you have to do something. You have to take advantage of the opportunities God sends you. You have to step into the boat. Do not miss the opportunities God sends you and drown because of your lack of action. Put your faith into action.

Follow David's Example of Faith

In this Chapter we have examined three things you need to do to help you go beyond your limits. You increase by setting goals. You increase by the words you speak. You increase by taking decisive action. In Chapter 2 we talked about how David triumphed over Goliath. David put his faith into action. David set a goal to kill the giant. David spoke to the giant and said what he was going to do to him. Then, David did what he said. Let us look more closely at these principles at work in David's triumph over Goliath.

David Set a Goal to Kill the Giant

David set a goal to kill the giant Goliath. David ana-
lyzed his circumstances. He assessed his risks and
rewards. He asked questions and found out that the man
who killed Goliath would receive financial rewards, freedom from taxes and the king's daughter in marriage.
David knew what the rewards would be when he accomplished his goal.

> And all the men of Israel, when they saw the
> man, fled from him, and were sore afraid. And the
> men of Israel said, Have ye seen this man that is
> come up? surely to defy Israel is he come up: and
> it shall be, that the man who killeth him, the king
> will enrich him with great riches, and will give him
> his daughter, and make his father's house free in
> Israel.
>
> And David spake to the men that stood by
> him, saying, What shall be done to the man that
> killeth this Philistine, and taketh away the
> reproach from Israel? for who is this uncircum-
> cised Philistine, that he should defy the armies of
> the living God?
>
> And the people answered him after this man-
> ner, saying, So shall it be done to the man that kil-
> leth him.   (1 Samuel 17:24-27).

David developed a plan. He took with him his staff,
his slingshot and five smooth stones. David prepared for
battle by taking familiar weapons. The king tried to give
David his bulky armor and sword. David did not take
them because he had not proved them in battle (1 Samuel
17:38-39). He knew how to use his staff and sling as effective weapons. Shepherds had to use them to defend their
flocks. David knew how to accurately sling stones, but he

was not used to a sword and armor. He chose weapons he knew how to use.

> And he took his staff in his hand, and chose him five smooth stones out of the brook, and put them in a shepherd's bag which he had, even in a scrip; and his sling was in his hand: and he drew near to the Philistine.
>
> And the Philistine came on and drew near unto David; and the man that bare the shield went before him. And when the Philistine looked about, and saw David, he disdained him: for he was but a youth, and ruddy, and of a fair countenance. And the Philistine said unto David, Am I a dog, that thou comest to me with staves? And the Philistine cursed David by his gods. And the Philistine said to David, Come to me, and I will give thy flesh unto the fowls of the air, and to the beasts of the field.   (1 Samuel 17:40-44).

David Spoke to the Giant

David told the giant he was going to kill him. This was no idle threat. David was experienced. He had already killed a lion and a bear while protecting his family's sheep (1 Samuel 17:34-37). David knew he was in covenant with God. He knew the giant, an uncircumcised Philistine, was not in covenant with God. David spoke faith-filled words. David knew God was able to help him defeat his enemies. David could boldly declare he was going to kill Goliath.

> Then said David to the Philistine, Thou comest to me with a sword, and with a spear, and with a shield: but I come to thee in the name of the LORD of hosts, the God of the armies of Israel, whom thou hast defied. This day will the LORD

> deliver thee into mine hand; and I will smite thee, and take thine head from thee; and I will give the carcases of the host of the Philistines this day unto the fowls of the air, and to the wild beasts of the earth; that all the earth may know that there is a God in Israel. And all this assembly shall know that the LORD saveth not with sword and spear: for the battle is the LORD'S, and he will give you into our hands. (1 Samuel 17:45-47).

David Put His Faith into Action

David did more than prepare to do battle and talk about it. He took immediate action. He followed through with his plan. David put his faith into action.

> And it came to pass, when the Philistine arose, and came and drew nigh to meet David, that David hasted, and ran toward the army to meet the Philistine. And David put his hand in his bag, and took thence a stone, and slang it, and smote the Philistine in his forehead, that the stone sunk into his forehead; and he fell upon his face to the earth. So David prevailed over the Philistine with a sling and with a stone, and smote the Philistine, and slew him; but there was no sword in the hand of David. Therefore David ran, and stood upon the Philistine, and took his sword, and drew it out of the sheath thereof, and slew him, and cut off his head therewith. And when the Philistines saw their champion was dead, they fled.
>
> (1 Samuel 17:48-51).

David believed God was going to help him and he put his faith into action. The Bible says David "hasted." In other words David was in a hurry to take out the giant. He ran toward the giant and slung one of the stones. He hit the giant right between the eyes and knocked him out. He took the giant's sword from him and cut his head off. David carried the giant's head around in triumph. The men of Israel were encouraged by David's triumph and they went on to win a great victory over the Philistine army.

When God helped David accomplish his goal, it brought great glory to God. David had a goal. He told the giant what he was going to do to him. David took decisive action. He succeeded in his goal, and then he triumphed over his enemy. If a teenager like David can triumph over his enemy, you can triumph over your problems and circumstances. It does not matter how young or how old you are, with the help of God, all things are possible for those who believe.

Put Your Faith into Action

You can apply action to your goals just like David. These principles will work for you in any area of life. These principles will work for anything: making financial investments, improving your marriage, increasing your ministry, etc. You can set goals, speak to your circumstances and take decisive action.

Follow through with your goals. Follow through with your words. God rewards those who put their faith in action. Faith with action is a live vital faith. Faith with action moves mountains and slays giants. Faith with action causes you to triumph and give glory to God.

OVERCOMING LIMITS DAILY

YOU LIVE LIFE DAILY

* * *

Tomorrow Never Comes

When I was in school at Henderson State College in Arkadelphia, Arkansas, I was not a Christian. I was lost just like most of the other students. Every Friday night, whenever we could, we would drive a few miles over to Hot Springs. One time we went to a pizza parlor. The pizza parlor had a sign that read, "Free Beer Tomorrow!" We saw that sign and decided we were going to come back to this place tomorrow and drink free beer. The next day we drove back to the pizza parlor. We went in and said, "We want our free beer." The owner looked at us, pointed at the sign, laughed and said, "It's tomorrow!"

We were college students, and we thought we were so smart, but we learned a valuable lesson that night. Today is always today and tomorrow is always the next day. Tomorrow never comes. When you wake-up tomorrow, it is not going to be tomorrow, it is going to be today.

Rejoice in the Day the Lord Has Made

Life brings us one day at a time. Forget the past. Do

not worry about tomorrow. Live your life one day at a time. Realize God is with you daily.

Living a life of faith is a daily thing. Faith is an invisible force that directs your life every day. Faith is not found in the future. Faith is not found in the past. Faith is always now. Faith is always in the present tense.

> Now faith is the substance of things hoped for,
> the evidence of things not seen. (Hebrews 11:1).

Today, God is working with you. Today, God is blessing you. Today, God has caused you to be an overcomer. Today, God has caused you to be triumphant in Christ. Today, God wants you to live and enjoy your life. Today is the day the Lord has made. Rejoice in the day He has given you and be glad (Psalm 118:24).

Everything You Do in Life Is Daily

Life is a daily process. You have to take action every day to remove the limits in your life. Do not wait for a crisis to overtake you. You should not wait until they back the truck up to your door and repossess your furniture to take action. You should not wait until the doctor says you have six months to live to take action. You should take care of your personal hygiene daily by bathing and brushing your teeth daily. You should not wait months or years to forgive a person who has you all bent out of shape. You have to remove the limits in your life starting now, today.

I say all this to make a point. Much of life is daily. God created you with daily needs. Even in creation God did things on a daily basis.

If you want to increase your physical limits, you need to exercise every day. If you start exercising daily, it may take you six months or a year to see results. You might be tempted to quit before you reach your goal. If you do not work at it daily, you will not succeed. Exercising once a month is not going to accomplish the results you are seeking. If you are going to increase your physical limits, you have to work at it daily.

GIVE US THIS DAY OUR DAILY BREAD

* * *

Pray Daily

In the Lord's Prayer, Jesus taught His disciples to pray for their daily needs. He taught them to pray for their bread every day.

> Give us this day our daily bread.
>
> (Matthew 6:11).

Bread can represent more than food. Bread can represent all the daily needs in your life. Bread also represents Jesus Himself. Jesus referred to Himself as the bread of life (John 6:35).

It should be as important to pray on a daily basis as it is to eat. If you eat every day, you should also pray every day. You need to enter into the presence of God every day with your prayers (Psalms 140:13).

The key to success in anything is to discipline yourself to do daily tasks related to your goals. Daily discipline is what sets champions apart from most other people. Praying on a daily basis will determine how effective you will be as an overcomer and champion in Christ. Praying daily is an important part of overcoming limits in your life.

Read and Study Your Bible Daily

Champions in Christ need to read and study the Word of God on a daily basis. The Word of God is taken into your spirit and provides fuel for spiritual power just like food provides the fuel for your physical body.

The first Psalm talks about the impact of daily Bible devotional readings. You should not delight in listening to ungodly counsel or to people with negative attitudes. You should delight in the word of God.

> Blessed is the man that walketh not in the counsel of the ungodly, nor standeth in the way of sinners, nor sitteth in the seat of the scornful. But his delight is in the law of the LORD; and in his law doth he meditate day and night. And he shall be like a tree planted by the rivers of water, that bringeth forth his fruit in his season; his leaf also shall not wither; and whatsoever he doeth shall prosper. (Psalms 1:1-3).

Daily Bible devotions feed and develop you spiritually. Spiritual growth requires taking the seed, the Word of God, and watering it daily. Fruit tree seeds take years to become trees. It takes years to become a mature Christian. After a fruit tree matures, it produces fruit. Spiritual growth will also produce fruit in its season. The key to spiritual growth is to feed and water yourself daily to provide the necessary nutrients to grow.

Joshua took over ruling the nation of Israel after Moses died. God used Joshua to take the nation of Israel from the desert, where they had wandered around for forty years, into their Promised Land. The Promised Land was full of enemies and Joshua had to lead the Israelites through many battles. He would not have been successful in achieving victory if he had not stayed connected to God daily. Moses had written the first five books of the Bible and left them with the Israelites. God told Joshua to read these books daily.

> This book of the law shall not depart out of
> thy mouth; but thou shalt meditate therein day
> and night, that thou mayest observe to do accord-
> ing to all that is written therein: for then thou shalt
> make thy way prosperous, and then thou shalt
> have good success.   (Joshua 1:8).

God told Joshua to meditate the Bible. Meditate does not mean to read quickly. Meditate means to read and consider what is being read. Meditating on the Word of God means to think about what you have read and then apply what you have read to your daily life.

Joshua was triumphant over his enemies. The Israelites, with God's help, conquered cities and established a nation based upon God's promise to them. If you are going to establish yourself and enjoy triumph over your spiritual enemies, you must read and study your Bible daily. You must base your life on God's Word.

Daily devotion to the Word of God is an important part of being a successful Christian. Daily Bible reading and study are essential for living a life with no more limits.

Do Not Worry About Daily Needs

Jesus taught His disciples to pray for their daily bread. He also taught them not to worry about where it was going to come from.

> Therefore take no thought, saying, What shall
> we eat? or, What shall we drink? or, Wherewithal
> shall we be clothed?   (Matthew 6:31).

When Jesus says to "take no thought," he is not saying to never think about or pray about what you are supposed to eat or drink. Taking no thought means not to worry about your food, drink or clothes. Jesus is saying not to be anxious about your needs. Jesus already taught them to pray and trust God for their daily bread. Jesus is now teaching them not to worry once they had prayed for their needs.

Anxious thoughts come to everybody. Some people seem to worry about everything. When you are worrying about your needs, you are failing to put God first in your life. When you are worrying about your basic needs, you are demonstrating a lack of confidence and trust in God's ability to meet your needs and to answer your prayers.

Jesus went on to tell His disciples to establish their priorities on God.

> But seek ye first the kingdom of God, and his righteousness; and all these things shall be added unto you.   (Matthew 6:33).

When you make God your number one priority in life, you will never have to worry or be anxious about what you are going to eat, drink or wear. God is going to provide these things for you when you pray.

Notice that Jesus said in Matthew 6:31 to take no thought saying, "What are we going to eat?" "What are we going to drink?" or "What are we going to wear?" Jesus is saying not to talk negatively. If you have faith in God, you should already know the answer to these questions. God is going provide your food! God is going to provide your drink! God is going to provide your clothes! Do not worry or question how or by whom these things will come. Seek God first and all these things will be provided for you in God's perfect way.

Receiving Peace for Daily Living

The Apostle Paul reinforced the Jesus' teaching about praying and not worrying. Paul said:

> Be careful for nothing; but in every thing by prayer and supplication with thanksgiving let your requests be made known unto God.
>
> (Philippians 4:6).

Paul said not to worry but to pray. Pray about everything that is bothering you. Let all your needs be known to God. After you ask God for your needs, give thanks that He hears your prayers. Give thanks that He knows your needs. Thank God for answering your prayers and do not worry about them after you pray.

Are you seeking God in your life? Is God your top priority? If you are obedient to Him and seeking Him, you will have your needs met.

If you pray, "God, I don't want limits in my life anymore." God says, "That is good. You are on the right track. I will help you."

If you pray, "God, I don't want to lose my temper anymore." God hears that and says, "I will help you."

If you pray, "God I am petitioning you, and I am thanking you right now that I am not going to be limited by fear anymore. I'm not going to worry, I'm not going to be anxious for anything." God says, "Keep it up. Keep petitioning me for your needs. Keep thanking me for it. Thank me for it everyday."

After you have made your requests and thanked God for answering your prayers, the Scripture goes on to say:

> And the peace of God, which passeth all understanding, shall keep your hearts and minds through Christ Jesus. (Philippians 4:7).

There is a release that comes from prayer. Once you pray with thanksgiving you do not need to worry. When you believe God has heard and answered your prayers, you will have peace. The worries are gone and peace floods your heart and mind.

Think Pure Thoughts

The next verse in Philippians tells you how to keep peace in your heart and mind. Once you have prayed, given thanks and received peace, you must take control of your thoughts.

Finally, brethren, whatsoever things are true, whatsoever things are honest, whatsoever things are just, whatsoever things are pure, whatsoever things are lovely, whatsoever things are of good report; if there be any virtue, and if there be any praise, think on these things. (Philippians 4:8).

Have you noticed that the things you worry about do not usually come to pass? Most of the time the things that you are worried about never happen.

Your mind might tell you the whole world is tumbling down around you. You might build up obstacles and limits in your mind that do not exist. Since most of these things will never happen, why worry about them? Replace those negative thoughts with positive thoughts.

The Bible says think on things that are good, just, honest and pure. Stop filling your mind with negative thoughts, and you will enjoy the peace God gives your heart and mind after you pray.

Overcoming Limits Daily

You have to live one day at a time. The word "disciple" means *disciplined one*. You have to be disciplined at seeking God. When you become disciplined, you are going to start seeing the results. You eat daily. You clean yourself daily. What you do for God, you should do daily. Disciplined people develop good daily habits. You should read your Bible and pray daily.

Do not despair if you miss it or make a mistake. I have exercised and pulled muscles. After time passed, I healed. I did not quit exercising because I hurt myself. I just stopped for a little while to heal, and then I started exercising again.

If you fall down and make a mistake, ask God to forgive you. You say, "Father, I am sorry. I repent. Please forgive me." Do what you need to do to make it right. Forgive yourself. Forget it and move on with your life.

You may have prayed like this: "Father, I am going to walk in your divine favor today. I'm not going to become upset today. I'm not going to be offended today. I'm going to walk in your perfect peace. I'm not going to be worried. Amen."

After you pray a prayer like this, you may go on about your daily business and, suddenly, a situation arises which could cause you to become upset and worry. You may have missed it yesterday and the day before, but this time something is different. You have been praying, and you have been reading your Bible daily. You have been keeping God first in your life. You have set a goal not to be angry and upset. You have prayed about it, and now you realize you are not angry or upset at this situation. Yesterday it bothered you, but today you have victory.

Whatever limits you may have in your life, if you continue to pray and read your Bible daily, you will find yourself conquering your limits. Spiritually, you will grow when you read your Bible and pray daily. A tree may not look like it is growing, but if it is healthy and receiving the proper nutrition and sunshine, it will grow. You are the same way. If you receive the proper spiritual nutrition and spiritual sunshine daily from the Bible, you will grow. Daily spiritual growth will help you reach new levels of Christian maturity. Those things that used to bother you will no longer hold you back. Your limits will be broken.

Living a life pleasing to God will remove limits in your life. Time will prove this true. Months from now, maybe even years from now, you will look back and see how you have changed. You will see how you have grown into a different person.

As you continue to grow on a daily basis, you will increase in many areas. Your tithe will increase. Your energy will increase. Your prayer life will increase. Your spiritual life will increase. Your strength will increase. You will be amazed at how many ways you have increased.

Living a triumphant daily life means you will keep expanding your boundaries. Living a triumphant daily life means you always glorify and please God. Living a triumphant daily life means your life is filled with joy. This is the way life with Jesus was intended to be lived — abundantly — a life without limits.